DESIGNING A LIFESTYLE THAT PLEASES GOD

A PRACTICAL GUIDE

PAT ENNIS & LISA TATLOCK

MOODY PUBLISHERS
CHICAGO

All Scripture quotations, unless otherwise indicated, are taken from the *New American Standard Bible®*, Copyright © The Lockman Foundation 1960, 1962, 1963, 1968, 1971, 1972, 1973, 1975, 1977, 1995. Used by permission.

Scripture quotations marked NKJV are taken from the *New King James Version*. Copyright © 1982, 1992 by Thomas Nelson, Inc. Used by permission. All rights reserved.

Scripture quotations marked KJV are taken from the King James Version.

Library of Congress Cataloging-in-Publication Data

Ennis, Pat.
    Designing a lifestyle that pleases God / Pat Ennis and Lisa Tatlock.
      p. cm.
    Includes bibliographical references.
    ISBN 0-8024-1421-4
     1. Christian women—Religious life. 2. Christian women—Conduct of life.
  3. Christian life—Biblical teaching. I. Tatlock, Lisa. II. Title.

BV4527.E565 2004
248.8'43—dc22

                                      2004008625

1 3 5 7 9 10 8 6 4 2

Printed in the United States of America

DESIGNING
A LIFESTYLE
THAT PLEASES
GOD

This book is dedicated to

Carella DeVol—Pat's roommate

*Your moral support, enthusiasm, and consistent prayer
on all aspects of my ministry are a constant source of blessing.*

A friend loves at all times . . .
Proverbs 17:17

ഔ ഔ ഔ ഔ ഔ

Mark Tatlock—Lisa's husband

*Visionary, faithful, compassionate, servant leader,
and an adverturesome spirit are all character traits
which encouraged me while writing this book.
It is my* **joy** *to strive to be an excellent wife for you!*

*A righteous man who walks in his integrity—
How blessed are his sons after him.*
Proverbs 20:7

CONTENTS

ACKNOWLEDGMENTS

We are indebted to the many individuals who supported the creation of *Designing a Lifestyle that Pleases God*. Among them we offer special gratitude to:

Drs. Tim LaHaye and John MacArthur—your vision to develop a character-based Home Economics curriculum and perpetuate it made this volume possible.

Elsa Mazon—your enthusiasm for both *Becoming a Woman Who Pleases God* and *Designing a Lifestyle that Pleases God* was evident from our initial contact. Thank you for presenting our proposal to the Leadership Team, responding to a myriad of questions, and for seeing the project through to its completion.

Dr. Barbara Schuch—your unselfish sharing of your editorial skills, thought-provoking comments, and belief in *Designing a Lifestyle that Pleases God* provided momentum to keep the project in process.

Elizabeth George—who gave sacrificially of her time to write the Foreword for us.

Our endorsers: Nancy Leigh DeMoss, Karina Alcorn Franklin, Patricia MacArthur, Martha Peace, and Dr. Stuart Scott—who not only supported the content of *Designing a Lifestyle that Pleases God,* but also our character.

The Designing a Lifestyle that Pleases God *team*—your commitment to excellence made this partnership in the ministry of the written Word a joy.

Amy Peterson—who fulfills her job title of Author Relations Manager to the fullest extent.

Ali Childers—what a joy to have you as our editor. Thank you for adhering to a high standard of excellence throughout the editing process.

Our students, both at Christian Heritage and The Master's College—your presence in our classes and completion of our assignments helped in the compilation of the synopsis of your Home Economics education.

Our Heavenly Father—YOU established the criteria for the lifestyle of the Christian woman in Your holy Word and then provide the strength to apply it to daily living. Eternity will not be long enough for us to express our love and gratitude to YOU!

FOREWORD

Dear Reader,

If you're like me, you are always on the lookout for a book that's a joy to read, contains life-changing information presented by someone who knows the subject inside and out, tells you how to apply its principles, and, of course, feeds you with God's rich and instructive Word.

Well, all I can say is, you've found it! What you hold in your hands is just such a book—and you're going to love it! Why? Because it has heart, and it gives you something you deeply desire—principles for living a life that pleases God—which you can apply immediately! Regardless of your age or the season of your life, this book will move you even further toward making your heart's desire to become a woman of great wisdom a reality.

Designing a Lifestyle that Pleases God is a powerful treasury of the timeless principles from the Bible for guiding a woman's life. In each chapter, my wonderful friends, Patricia Ennis and Lisa Tatlock, share about life issues that women face on a daily basis. And they do so by drawing from the wealth of not one, but two lifetimes of wisdom and experience. These servants of God have each sought, by His grace, to live a lifestyle that pleases God. Plus they have been teaching the biblical principles that can make this a reality through one-on-one mentoring relationships, in small groups, in large church settings, and as faculty members at The Master's College.

It is with great joy that I recommend this book to you. You see, I know the authors, their hearts, their lives, their families, and their golden credentials. And I've seen the fruit of their labor. I know hundreds of women who have personally been touched and changed for life by the influence of these two knowledgeable mentors and the godly wisdom they so graciously share with women like you and me.

This treasure of a book and the biblical principles it presents will definitely help *you* to fulfill your dream of designing a lifestyle that pleases God. And, oh, what glory He will receive as you seek to do so!

In His love,
ELIZABETH GEORGE

DESIGNING A LIFESTYLE THAT PLEASES GOD

The purpose of *Designing a Lifestyle that Pleases God* is to encourage you to pursue the biblical principles found in Titus 2:3–5, a passage that identifies biblical priorities for Christian women. A companion volume to *Becoming a Woman Who Pleases God,* our book's message focuses on developing both the Christian character and ways of living depicted in Titus 2.

The content of *Designing a Lifestyle that Pleases God* is based on a portion of the curriculum of the Home Economics Department at The Master's College and includes several of the topics frequently requested by individuals who are unable to enroll as students. These topics include: financial management, hospitality, interior design, and clothing selection. Home Economics at The Master's College is unique because of "the integration of faith and learning," meaning that our students receive professional training while studying the biblical priorities that prepare them to fulfill their God-ordained roles.

The phrase "Wise Woman" is used throughout this book to emphasize that women who practice the principles found in God's Word are women who have both understood and applied the truths found in God's Word.

Though we each could have written this book independently, we worked together because we believed that it would be a more useful resource if we each contributed our strengths. We are two very different individuals, but our common commitment to the truths found in Titus 2 and the discipline of Home Economics resulted in the development of an intimate friendship as well as a unique professional team. Pat began teaching at the college level in 1976 and Lisa in 1988.

Pat wrote chapters 1, 2, 4, 7, and 10. Chapter one identifies key principles from Proverbs 31 and poses the question, "Am I a Christian woman or a woman who is a Christian?" Chapter two focuses on God's special instructions to women, while chapter four encourages the Wise Woman to view her career as a high calling from her heavenly Father. Chapter seven motivates the Wise Woman to cultivate a heart for hospitality, and chapter ten concludes the book with a discussion of how to practice the principles outlined for Wise Women in 1 Peter 3:1–9.

Lisa wrote chapters 3, 5, 6, 8, and 9. Chapter three paints a word picture of biblical submission, while chapter five challenges the Wise Woman to pursue motherhood with excellence. Chapter six builds on the principles of stewardship introduced in *Becoming a Woman Who Pleases God* and offers tips for becoming a responsible consumer. Chapter eight provides the tools for creating a beautiful home, while chapter nine describes the keys to dressing with discernment.

Each chapter concludes with follow-up "growth projects," which provide the reader with an opportunity to personally apply the chapter's content. It is our prayer that as you read through *Designing a Lifestyle that Pleases God* you will be motivated to become a woman who wisely builds her home (Proverbs 14:1) and that you will be encouraged to live out with excellence the principles found in Titus 2.

The July sun shined brightly as I parked my car at Lisa's and gathered my resources. She emerged from her front door to check her mailbox, and we walked up her front walk together. Her "little men," Jacob and Josiah, were sleeping, and we had several hours of uninterrupted talk time. I could not believe that we were really meeting with the intention of talking about a second book—we had just recently sent our final manuscript for Becoming a Woman Who Pleases God to our publisher.

The impact of the morning we had sent off the completed manuscript of our first book was still etched on my heart. When I had started my car to drive to The Master's College campus to make the final copies and deliver the manuscript to the campus mailroom, our town's Christian radio station was playing "To God Be the Glory." I wept as I drove down the hill. Truly, the completed work had only been possible because of HIM (which is the way we wanted it)!! Between Lisa and me, I think Satan had tried every trick in his book to slow our progress and discourage us—and yet our gracious heavenly Father had allowed us to finish HIS book two weeks before our publisher's deadline.

People had repeatedly asked if we had started our second book. Each time we had searched for a gracious response. We had thought *we might have said all that needed saying in* Becoming a Woman Who Pleases God. *However, we were asked the question enough times to realize our heavenly Father could be sowing the seed for a companion volume. Thus the reason for our afternoon meeting—to prayerfully consider a second volume.*

Lisa's prepared home and tender prayer set the tone for our time together; we were each prepared with suggested topics. Two hours later her "little men" were awake, and the Lord had already provided a title, purpose statement, chapter format, and content ideas. We each had our writing assignments that would focus on Designing a Lifestyle that Pleases God *beginning with the foundation that ...*

THE WISE WOMAN'S LIFESTYLE REFLECTS HER HEAVENLY HERITAGE

Then God said,
"Let Us make man in Our image,
according to Our likeness."
GENESIS 1:26

As we begin this chapter, let me ask you a question—"Are you a Christian woman or a woman who is a Christian?" On the surface, both appear to be identical. However, it is one thing to describe yourself as a Christian, and it is another thing to *be* one through and through. A woman can call herself Christian but not really live according to scriptural guidelines and be transformed by the Spirit of God. She may be theologically sound but practically inept; and as James teaches, Christians are to, "prove yourselves doers of the word, and not merely hearers who delude themselves" (James 1:22). The second portion of the question describes the woman who, by her lifestyle, clearly demonstrates that her values and character align with the Word of God. Let's take a look at what God's Word says as you consider your response to my question!

A SNAPSHOT OF THE WISE WOMAN

The wise woman builds her house,
But the foolish tears it down with her own hands.
PROVERBS 14:1

In the first chapter of *Becoming a Woman Who Pleases God* we introduced the woman whose lifestyle, values, and character align with the Word of God.[1] We established that Proverbs 31:10–31 paints a word portrait of the character of the woman who is a Christian. We twenty-first-century women are challenged to follow her example. The immutability of God is in question if Proverbs 31:10–31 is not relevant. We looked at the six attributes of God that provide a solid foundation for our study of Scripture:

- God's life does not change.
- God's character does not change.
- God's truth does not change.
- God's ways do not change.
- God's purposes do not change.
- God's SON does not change.[2]

Since God is immutable, a Wise Woman cultivates a lifestyle that reflects that she believes His principles are essentially the same realities for twenty-first-century Christians as they were for those of the Old and New Testaments. We learned that the description of the Wise Woman of Proverbs 31:10–31 is not designed to develop an inferiority complex within us—rather it provides a biblical foundation for the creation of principles by which we, as Wise Women in progress, prioritize our lives.

We then examined eleven characteristics of Wise Women—
Virtuous, Trustworthy, Energetic, Physically Fit, Economical, Un-
selfish, Honorable, Lovable, Prepared, Prudent, and God-fearing.
Let's take a moment to reflect on the heart of these principles:

- *Virtuous* (31:10) describes an inner quality that instinc-
  tively demands respect. Moral excellence characterizes all
  of this woman's behavior (Ruth 3:11).
- *Trustworthy* (31:11–12) is indicative of the ability to keep
  another's confidence. Our Wise Woman's speech is encouraging, sympathetic, and tactful (Proverbs 25:11). Her
  love of the Lord is evident (John 14:15), and dependability
  is exhibited in her lifestyle (Proverbs 25:13).
- *Energetic* (31:13–16, 19, 24, 27) suggests that our Wise
  Woman is a worker and not a shirker (Proverbs 10:4). Her
  Christianity is practical (James 1:17); she enjoys her work
  (John 4:36), and attacks it with a cheery attitude (Colossians 3:17).
- *Physically Fit* (31:17) reminds us that to perform our du-
  ties efficiently we must be healthy. As Wise Women in
  progress we seek to understand our personal limitations
  and then work within them (1 Corinthians 6:19).
- *Economical* (31:18) challenges our wise woman to refrain
  from wasting time, money, fuel, or any other resource. She
  operates her home on a budget (a plan for spending) and
  at the end of the month there is not "too much month
  left at the end of the money."
- *Unselfish* (31:20) depicts her willingness to share her most
  valuable asset—her time—with others. Practically speaking, a Wise Woman is not so busy with her own affairs
  that she can't lend a helping hand to others. Her words
  bring comfort, hope, cheer, and, when necessary, correction to those who touch her life (Galatians 6:10).
- *Honorable* (31:25) characterizes her choice to "abstain

from every form of evil" (1 Thessalonians 5:22). She dresses modestly and understands the importance of maintaining a reputation of integrity (Proverbs 22:1).

- *Lovable* (31:28–29) embodies the consistency of her lifestyle. She enjoys relationships that have depth because she seeks to sharpen her friends spiritually and intellectually (Proverbs 27:17).

- *Prepared* (31:21–22) includes our Wise Woman's ability to cope with unforeseen circumstances with confidence (Philippians 4:13).

- *Prudent* (31:26) implies that our Wise Woman is practically wise and careful of the consequences; that is, she is cautious. As she speaks she has the ability to be firm, yet kind (Proverbs 27:9).

- *God-fearing* (31:30) suggests that her actions and lifestyle consistently reflect that she stands in awe of the Lord (Proverbs 1:7) and loves Him with all of her heart (Matthew 22:37).

We then examined Proverbs 31:31 which describes *the reward* of cultivating the eleven principles. The Wise Woman receives her rewards "in the gates," which refers to the public assembly of people; she is often rewarded in this life and always in the hereafter (1 Corinthians 3:10–15; 4:1–21; 5:10; Revelation 22:12).

"Jesus said, 'You were faithful over a few things, I will make you ruler over many things'" (Matthew 25:21 NKJV). He meant that a person who is faithful in serving the Lord here would be rewarded with an honored position in His millennial kingdom.[3] Our Wise Woman lives in such a way that Jesus' words in Matthew 25:21 characterize her daily life.

THE WISE WOMAN PURSUES WISDOM

The beginning of wisdom is:

Acquire wisdom;
And with all your acquiring, get understanding.
PROVERBS 4:7

Becoming a Wise Woman was the theme of *Becoming a Woman Who Pleases God,* as it is in this volume. The book of Proverbs reminds us repeatedly that if we choose to live wisely, our lives can be rich and abundant now, as they will be forever in eternity. First Kings 3:3–15 describes a prayer of Solomon's which serves as a model for all Wise Women in progress:

1. Solomon loved the Lord and walked in the statutes of his father, David (3:3).
2. He was privileged to experience a unique, two-way conversation with the Lord (3:5).
3. He viewed his succession to David as evidence of the Lord's faithfulness to His promises to his father (3:6).
4. He humbly admitted his inadequate qualifications for the position the Lord asked him to assume (3:7).
5. He petitioned the Lord for an understanding heart to judge His people (3:9).
6. He received what he did not ask for (riches and honor) because he sought God's wisdom first (3:13).

Application of Solomon's prayer for twenty-first-century women may include:

1. Loving the Lord completely (Mark 12:30).
2. Communing with God through prayer (Philippians 4:6–7; 1 Thessalonians 5:17).
3. Believing that her heavenly Father will complete the good work He has begun in her (Philippians 1:6).
4. Understanding that she can only complete her Father's work through His strength (Philippians 4:13).

5. Seeking the Lord's wisdom rather than relying on her knowledge and experiences (James 1:5).
6. Trusting that God's ways are best (Proverbs 3:5–6).

While embracing the positive attributes exhibited by Solomon, our Wise Woman will be careful to avoid the fatal errors that were a part of his character. Though he walked in the statutes of his father and loved the Lord, his choice to continually worship at the high places demonstrated that he failed to follow Him completely (1 Kings 3:3). As well, he chose to live life on his own terms rather than personally applying the truth. A Wise Woman identifies the "high places" in her life, and she seeks, through God's strength, to "utterly destroy" them (Deuteronomy 12:1–7). She purposes to skillfully apply biblical truth to practical living (James 4:17).

THE WISE WOMAN IS GRACIOUS

A gracious woman attains honor.
PROVERBS 11:16

Gracious is a word that we don't hear very often anymore. Biblically, the word *gracious* describes one who has a kind disposition and shows favor and mercy to another. For example, Boaz showed favor to Ruth (Ruth 2:10), and King Ahasureus' treated Esther graciously (Esther 2:17; 5:2).[4] It is worth mentioning that these women treated these men with kindness and gentleness from the start, which in turn led to favor being bestowed upon them. Practically speaking, a gracious woman will be pleasant, kind, merciful, compassionate, and characterized by good taste.

Our heavenly Father sets the model for graciousness toward others in Exodus 34:6: "The Lord, the Lord God, compassionate and gracious, slow to anger, and abounding in lovingkindness and truth." Psalm 86:15 (NKJV) portrays God as "full of compassion, and gracious, longsuffering and abundant in mercy and truth." Psalm 103:8 (NKJV) declares, "The Lord is merciful and gracious, slow to anger, and abounding in mercy," and Psalm 145:8 (NKJV) affirms, "The Lord is gracious and full of compassion, slow to anger and great in mercy."

The book of Proverbs provides several strategies for the integration of graciousness into the Wise Woman's life. She extends graciousness to the poor and needy (Proverbs 14:21, 31; 19:17), speaks *graciously* (Proverbs 22:11), and exemplifies graciousness in her behavior (Proverbs 11:6). John MacArthur's analysis of Proverbs 11:16 suggests, "While evil men may grasp at wealth, they will never attain the honor due a gracious woman."[5] Elizabeth George assists us in understanding the characteristics of a gracious tongue:

> Suppose you were in the presence of a woman who was thinking about God and enjoying sweet communion with Him as her thoughts ascended to His throne in prayer, who was continually absorbed in some portion of God's Holy Word, who was perhaps humming a hymn of praise to God. If you began to talk to one another, what do you imagine would come out of her mouth?

> I think you can safely answer something like this: You would hear words of blessing, words filled with graciousness and sweetness from such a woman. Tumbling forth from her lips would be soothing, healing words of comfort or uplifting encouragement, whichever was appropriate. Certainly you would witness words of mercy, concern, and compassion.[6]

The adjective *gracious* is found five times in the New Testament. The noun *grace* is used some 155 times, usually to describe what God did for us in Christ (Romans 5:2, 15, 17; 1 Corinthians 15:10, and Ephesians 1:20). The five instances of *gracious* provide a challenge for our Wise Woman and are worth taking a look at:

- Luke 4:22 reports that *all* who heard Jesus speak in the synagogue wondered at the *gracious* words that proceeded from His mouth.
- Luke 7:42 describes the *gracious* forgiveness of the moneylender to his two debtors.
- Romans 11:5 explains that because of God's *gracious* choice a remnant of Israel would come to faith in Him.
- Second Corinthians 8:6–7 refers to the *gracious* Macedonians' work of giving and urges that the Corinthians' giving align with them.
- Second Corinthians 8:19 refers to the Corinthians' *gracious* work of giving that was urged in 2 Corinthians 8:6–7.

Practical application of these verses finds our Wise Woman:

- always seeking to speak *graciously,*
- completely forgiving the wrongs of others,
- willingly sharing her faith,
- practicing generosity, and
- prayerfully considering others' urging of her generosity.

Recently one of our Home Economics graduates married the son of one of our seminary professors. The wedding ceremony was held in Georgia, the home state of the bride. Since the bride and groom reside in California, the groom's parents hosted a dinner reception in their California home several weeks later.

Since I know the groom's mother, Karen, I offered to help with the serving and cleanup of the reception. The gracious spirit Karen exemplified as she executed the lovely occasion blessed me. Her choices that serve as a model to all women desiring to be gracious hostesses include:

- She was willing to allow others to help. So many women have such a "Martha" complex that they are unwilling to allow others to share in the labor of an event. Work-ing together is often what builds strong relationships.

- She had written instructions and diagrams that eliminated the need to interrupt her when she needed to be with her guests.
- Once she gave an instruction, she allowed her helpers to follow through on the task without hovering over them.
- She was careful to express her gratitude.

The Wise Woman will be excited about integrating *graciousness* in her own life, as well as training others to follow her role model.

THE WISE WOMAN'S WALK

Therefore be careful how you walk,
not as unwise men, but as wise,
making the most of your time,
because the days are evil.
EPHESIANS 5:15–16

Our study of the Wise Woman teaches us a significant char-acter quality. Her heart is open to learning from the wisdom and experience of others. Biblical wisdom "is both religious and practical. Stemming from the fear of the Lord (Job 28:28; Psalm 111:10; Proverbs 1:7; 9:10), it branches out to touch all of life, as the extended commentary on wisdom in Proverbs indicates."[7] Wisdom takes insights gleaned from the knowledge of God's Word and applies it to one's daily walk. We know the Scrip-tures provide the basis for possessing a teachable heart (Proverbs 2:10–11), and we are reminded of Paul's teaching in 1 Corinthi-ans 10:6 (NKJV) that "now these things became our examples, to the intent that we should not lust after evil things as they [the Israelites] also lusted." Solomon's admonition that "fools despise wisdom and instruction" is a serious warning to us

(Proverbs 1:7 NKJV). However, once we are convinced that we need to seriously consider the wisdom of mature saints, our next step is to examine our daily walk. We will use an acrostic for the word *Christian* to look at day-to-day living:

C would of course stand for Christ. Women who ponder the answer to this question have learned about Him in their churches, Bible studies, and personal devotions. They know how to achieve salvation (Romans 3:10, 23; 5:8, 12; 6:23; 10:9, 10, 13). The significance of this part of the question is, does she just know about Christ, or does she know Him as her Lord and Savior (Matthew 7:13–23)?

H reminds us to be holy as God is holy (Leviticus 20:7). Do we fill our minds with thoughts that will challenge us to live a holy lifestyle (Philippians 4:8–9)?

R stands for reputation. People remember us by the things that we do. Throughout the Bible, Rahab was known as "Rahab the harlot" (Joshua 2:1; 6:22; Hebrews 11:31; James 2:25); though her lifestyle changed, her reputation followed her. Do I purpose to cultivate a reputation that invites others to imitate me as I imitate Christ (1 Corinthians 11:1)?

I focuses on integrity, a word that basically means that I choose to do what is right when given a choice between right and wrong. Those with integrity are allowed to dwell with the Lord (Psalm 15:2). Am I a person of integrity?

S stands for the Scriptures, God's Word, that has all of the answers to all of life's questions. However, they only answer the questions if they are diligently searched (John 5:39). Study of passages like Psalm 119 reveals all that God's Word will do for me. Do I live like I believe it?

T focuses our thoughts on our theme verses of Titus 2:4–5 (NKJV), where the older women are told to "admonish the young women to love their husbands, to love their children, to be discreet, chaste, homemakers, good, obedient to their own husbands, that the word of God may not be blasphemed." This passage implies that a young woman ought to learn how to manage her time and family finances, cook nutritious meals, practice hospitality, joyfully submit to her husband, and raise her children in the "training and admonition of the Lord" (Ephesians 6:4 NKJV) so that the Word of God will not be discredited. Am I willing to learn these skills and then teach others?

I directs the Wise Woman to inquire, in other words, to ask. Matthew 7:7–8 are two of the many verses that tell us that if we ask, our Lord will respond. Do I ask with a humble heart that is truly desirous of my heavenly Father's will?

A represents a challenge to abstain. Simply stated, abstain tells the Wise Woman to stay away from anything that could possibly not be good for her. First Thessalonians 5:22 is a short but potent verse that basically says anything that is unbiblical should be shunned! Do I abstain from every form of evil?

N reminds the Wise Woman that NOTHING is impossible when we trust our God. Proverbs 3:5–6 instructs us to place our trust in the Lord and not our own understanding—then our paths will be straight. Philippians 4:13 is a reminder that, through Christ, we can do all things. Do I trust God or lean on my own understanding?

THE WISE WOMAN'S RESPONSE

If indeed you have heard Him
and have been taught in Him,
just as truth is in Jesus, that, in reference
to your former manner of life,
you lay aside the old self,

which is being corrupted in accordance
with the lusts of deceit,
and that you be renewed in the spirit of your mind,
and put on the new self, which in
the likeness of God has been created
in righteousness and holiness of the truth.
EPHESIANS 4:21–24

We began this chapter by posing this question: "Are you a Christian woman or a woman who is a Christian?" As we viewed the Wise Woman's literary photo album, we found that a woman who is a Christian believes that the verbal picture of God's ideal woman painted in Proverbs 31:10–31 is as relevant today as the day it was written. Daily she seeks to be virtuous, trustworthy, energetic, physically fit, economical, unselfish, honorable, lovable, prepared, prudent, God-fearing, and rewarded. We found that she desires to model God's graciousness and eagerly learns from the experience and wisdom of others. She intentionally acquires instruction that allows her to use time management skills in her home, manage the family finances, cook nutritious meals, practice hospitality, joyfully submit to her husband, and raise her children in the "training and admonition of the Lord" so that God's Word will not be discredited.

Additionally, our Wise Woman seeks to develop the *gentle* and *quiet* spirit, which is precious to God. Peter challenges women in 1 Peter 3:1–6 to concentrate on developing chaste conduct (purity of life with reverence for God) rather than an incessant preoccupation with outward adornment. The "gentle and quiet spirit" is beauty that never decays as the outward body does. *Gentle* is actually "meek or humble," while *quiet* describes the character of a woman's action and reaction to life in general. We will explore the 1 Peter 3 passage in chapter ten as we investigate beauty that endures, establish a lasting standard of beauty, and learn that Christ is our role model for developing a "gentle and quiet spirit."

A Christian Woman may desire the benefit of being God's child but lack the motivation to integrate into her lifestyle the values and character that align with the Word of God. Ezekiel 33:30–33 describes this type of woman—she hears the Word of God, but her heart goes after covetousness (she wants God on her terms); consequently she chooses to ignore God's teaching to her. James 1:22 challenges women to be doers of the Word and not simply hearers.

Which part of my original question describes you?

A FINAL THOUGHT . . .

The lifestyle of God's Wise Woman reflects her heavenly heritage and focuses on the development of what is truly permanent and noteworthy—her character. This chapter concludes with a scriptural blueprint for designing the character of a woman who is a Christian, modeled after 1 Corinthians 13.

THE CHARACTER OF
A WOMAN WHO IS A CHRISTIAN

If I speak to other women about their scriptural roles and responsibilities but lack the motivation to integrate the teaching into my life, I am arrogant (James 2:22–25).

And though I know about the women of the Bible and believe myself to be a devoted Christian but fail to emulate their model, I am nothing (1 Corinthians 10:11).

If I pursue Christian ministry and stay up all night preparing a theologically correct Bible study but fail to develop the gentle and quiet spirit that is precious to my heavenly Father, my efforts are in vain (1 Peter 3:4).

A woman who is a Christian is gracious (Proverbs 11:16) even when others are not.

She believes that the verbal picture of God's ideal woman painted in Proverbs 31:10–31 is as relevant today as the day it was written and seeks to emulate her qualities.

A woman who is a Christian gleans insight from the knowledge of God's Word and seeks to become a Wise Woman (Proverbs 2:17–21).

She takes seriously the mandate of Titus 2:3–5 and intentionally acquires godly Christian role models and seeks to be one to those younger in the faith.

As for professional contacts, ultimately they will diminish in importance; as for speaking opportunities, they will be presented and the content eventually forgotten; as for strategic social events, they will occur and the memories will fade; but the woman who is a Christian prepares to face God's plan for her future with confidence (Proverbs 31:25).

So, both the Christian Woman and the woman who is a Christian abide in the Christian community; however, the woman who is a Christian cultivates a lifestyle that clearly displays that her values and character align with the Word of God.

GROWING IN
CHRISTIAN CHARACTER

1. Evaluate your lifestyle . . .

    a. Use specific examples to describe how you are faithful in serving the Lord here so you will be rewarded with an honored position in His millennial kingdom.

    b. Set personal goals that will challenge you to live in such a way that our Lord will say of you, "well done" (Matthew 25:21).

    c. Identify any "high places" in your life. Develop a strategy to "utterly destroy" them (Deuteronomy 12:1–7) through our Lord's strength and to skillfully apply biblical truth to practical living (James 4:17).

    d. Ask a Christian sister to hold you accountable to achieving the goals you established in steps b and c.

2. Consider each of the questions posed in the Christian acrostic. Write your response to each.

3. Study Psalm 119 and make a list of the things that God's Word can do in your life.

    a. Select the five areas that are difficult for you to surrender to the Lord. Write out verses that will remind you to trust God with those areas.

    b. Place them in a prominent place. Purpose to memorize and meditate upon the verses when you are tempted to be anxious instead of trusting (Philippians 4:6–7).

4. Develop your own acrostic for the word Christian. *Support each word with appropriate Scriptures.*

5. Set personal goals that will challenge you to activate the goals. As with question 1, ask a Christian sister to hold you accountable to achieving in these goals.

As I transitioned from teaching Proverbs 31:10-31 to a New Testament counterpart, I began reading at 1 Peter 2:21 to put the 1 Peter 3:1-12 passage in context. As I reached 1 Peter 3:7 (NKJV), out of the corner of my eye I observed one of my student's body language change dramatically after the phrase "a weaker vessel" was read. She was visibly displeased with the content. Knowing the student well, I was confident that as soon as I completed the reading she would have her hand raised—and my intuition was correct.

Having taught for a number of years, I have learned to pray and think on my feet. As I acknowledged the student, I petitioned my heavenly Father for His response to her straightforward statement, "I resent being labeled as weaker!"

God graciously provided my response by "fast forwarding" my eyes to the section of my notes that related to the verse, and I responded to her with these words:

> Peter provides a clear description of the attributes of godly living in the home and church in 1 Peter 3:1-12. He begins by describing the behavior that God expects of every wife in relationship to her husband (1 Peter 3:1-6) and concludes with the relationship that should exist among Christians, in general (1 Peter 3:8-12).

Sandwiched between the role of the wife and the relationship of Christians in general is 1 Peter 3:7—a verse which provides the foundation for lasting harmony in the home. Three specific principles emerge from this verse:

- The husband is to live with the wife in an understanding way.
- The husband is to honor his wife.
- The husband and wife share a joint inheritance as heirs together "of the grace of life."

Peter's use of the word likewise when addressing wives and husbands links this instruction with the example of Christ's sacrificial and unjust suffering given in the previous section of 1 Peter 2:21-25.

Peter instructs the husband to honor his wife; she is to be treated with esteem and dignity. As with a weaker vessel does not suggest an inferior position, but rather one used for a special purpose. Fine china is not used for camping—not because it is inferior, but rather because it is designed for more elegant occasions.

So the wife is not an inferior vessel, but rather one designed for a unique role.

Peter's final instruction to husbands is a word of warning—recognize your wife as a fellow heir or your prayers will be hindered! Peter recognized that marriage is a reciprocal, not a one-sided relationship. As husbands and wives acknowledge one another as joint heirs together of the grace of life, they will realize God's highest plan for their relationship.

As I completed my brief summary her body language relaxed, and she replied, "Oh, that makes sense—I am not inferior, but simply designed for a different use." I inwardly thanked my heavenly Father for His response, and continued the introduction to the content that would teach my students that . . .

THE WISE WOMAN UNDERSTANDS AND APPLIES GOD'S SPECIAL INSTRUCTIONS TO WOMEN

God created man in His own image,
in the image of God He created him;
male and female He created them.

GENESIS 1:27

If we are going to be known as Wise Women, we will make designing a lifestyle that pleases our heavenly Father our top priority. To cultivate such a lifestyle means that we must think like Him, and to think like Him we must have His mind. Proverbs 1:7 explains how to know our heavenly Father's mind—we reverence Him. As John MacArthur describes, "This reverential awe and admiring, submissive fear is foundational for all spiritual knowledge and wisdom. The fear of the Lord is a state of mind in which one's own attitudes, will, feelings, deeds and goals are exchanged for God's."[1] If we do not do this, then we are vulnerable to assimilating the fraudulent standards of man's wisdom. The voices of twenty-first-century society shout loudly to us to free or liberate ourselves from the bondage of our ancestors, "do our own thing," demand equality, gain personal fulfillment in life regardless of the impact on others, take control of our bodies, and many other things contrary to God's instructions. Moody Bible Institute President Joseph Stowell explains:

> It's not that freedom is so wrong. Scripture validates the pursuit of freedom. Yet it directs the pursuit in a surprisingly different way. As Christ says, true freedom begins with restrictions.

> We find this surprising definition of freedom in John 8:31–32, where Jesus says, "If you hold to my teaching, you are really my disciples. Then you will know the truth, and the truth will set you free." Notice the sequence. True freedom is not doing whatever I wish. Freedom is the result of my actualizing Christ's teaching, of restricting my life to that which is right and true.[2]

The Bible is clear that God's general purpose for all Christians is to be conformed to the image of Christ (Romans 8:29), bear fruit (John 15:1–11), walk by the Spirit (Galatians 5:16–26), exhibit conduct that reflects their salvation (Ephesians 4:1–3), be good stewards of all of their resources (1 Timothy 6:17–19), and eagerly anticipate His return (2 Timothy 4:8). As Wise Women we will not only cultivate a lifestyle that reflects God's general purpose, but also we will eagerly search the Scriptures to discover His special instructions to us.

THE WISE WOMAN SEARCHES FOR GOD'S SPECIAL INSTRUCTIONS TO WOMEN

Be diligent to present yourself approved to God
as a workman who does not need to be ashamed,
accurately handling the word of truth.

But avoid worldly and empty chatter,
for it will lead to further ungodliness.
2 TIMOTHY 2:15–16

You will recall that chapter one focused on the reality that the immutability of God is in question if Proverbs 31:10–31 is not relevant to our twenty-first-century lifestyle. This reality is true for all of the Scriptures that provide instruction for designing a lifestyle that allows us to be "doers of the word, and not merely hearers who delude themselves" (James 1:22). When we search the Scriptures, we uncover special instructions provided for us by our heavenly Father that a Wise Woman is:

- Aware that she was made by God in His own image (Genesis 1:27).
- A companion, helper, and an equal to her husband (Genesis 2:18, 21–24).
- Gracious (Proverbs 11:16).
- Discreet (Proverbs 11:22).
- The crown of her husband (Proverbs 12:4).
- Careful to build her house following the way of wisdom described in Proverbs 9:1–6 (Proverbs 14:1).
- The opposite of the contentious wife described throughout the book of Proverbs (Proverbs 19:13; 21:9, 19; 25:24; 27:15–16).
- An asset to her husband (Proverbs 18:22; 19:14).
- Worthy of praise (Ruth 3:11; Proverbs 31:10–31).
- Cautious to avoid cultivating the behaviors associated with a seductress (Ecclesiastes 7:26–28).
- Guarded in her behavior to prevent acquiring a reputation like the daughters of Zion (Isaiah 3:16–24).
- Submissive to her husband (Ephesians 5:22–23).
- Modest; her clothing reflecting that her heart is focused on

God—especially for worship (1 Timothy 2:9—see chapter ten).

- Trustworthy in all aspects of her life and ministry (1 Timothy 3:11).
- Willing to help widows who are in need (1 Timothy 5:1–16).
- Grounded in the Word of God (2 Timothy 3:6–7).
- Careful to develop a personal testimony that is consistent with her profession of faith (1 Timothy 2:10).
- Teachable (1 Timothy 2:11).
- Eager to train her children (2 Timothy 1:5).
- Available to teach the younger women (Titus 2:3–5).
- Excited about developing the type of character that pleases her heavenly Father (1 Peter 3:1–6).
- Faithful to follow the examples of the women who walk through the pages of the Old and New Testament (1 Corinthians 10:6; Hebrews 11:11; 1 Peter 3:1–6).

Perhaps the poem that follows, written by one of my students, will help you to direct your thoughts to the long-term benefits of obeying God's special instructions to you—even when they are contrary to popular trends.

Did They Know?

Contentious Sarah, did she know
That her plan could only bring woe?
But as she lived by God's rich grace
She would be the mother of a race.

Sinful Rahab, did she know
As she hid the spies, and kept them low,
She would be freed from her awful vice
And her name be found in the line of Christ?

Faithful Ruth, did she know
As she stayed by Naomi long ago,
Her kinsman redeemer, salvation would bring,
And she would become the mother of kings?

Lovely Esther, did she know
While in the palace, more beautiful to grow,
God would grant her that highest station,
And use her to rescue His chosen nation?

Favored Mary, did she know
As she lived her life humble and low,
That God would make her exalted among women,
And allow her to bear His Son from heaven?

Widow Anna, did she know
As her life to the service of God bestowed;
Her fastings and prayers were but a small price,
For the privilege of seeing God's Holy Christ?

Barren Elizabeth, did she know
As her husband prepared to the temple to go;
That he would return with a story of joy—
God would grant them a special little boy?

Godly Eunice, did she know
As she guided her son more Christ-like to grow;
That he would be used, beloved friend of Paul,
To bring many to Christ, redeemed from the fall?

෨

And you, dear woman, do you know
On the embers of your faith God will blow?
That child to raise, or that gap to span,
He will use them all to further His plan![3]

Though I grew up in a Christian home and thought I accepted Christ at the age of ten at Vacation Bible School, I did not mature as His disciple. As I entered my teen years and my elderly parents' health declined, I acquired a negative, cynical outlook on life. My father passed away during the first week of my freshman year of college, and my mother followed on my second day as a new teacher. I recall my pastor putting his arm around me at my mother's funeral and saying, "We'll see you in church on Sunday." Outwardly, I simply nodded my head, while inwardly I thought, "I have attended church since I was an infant; it has done nothing for me, and I have better things to do with my Sundays."

As I settled into my role as a new professional, my life *appeared* ideal—I had a good job, a boyfriend, and discretionary financial resources for the first time in my life, a compatible roommate, and was in an upward career track in my profession. Despite all of the "good things" that were happening externally, I experienced an internal, gnawing hunger. I vividly recall returning home from a date one Friday night and saying to my roommate, "I don't know what you are doing Sunday, but I am going to church." Since she didn't have other plans she agreed to attend with me. I did not want to return to my childhood church, so we attended one about a mile from home. Tim LaHaye was the pastor, and before we left the church that Sunday, individually, we both made certain that we were a part of God's family (see Romans 3:10, 23; 5:8, 12; 6:23; 10:9–11, 13).

As an educated woman, I was excited to both learn from a gifted pastor and study the Word of God on my own (Pastor

LaHaye consistently repeated, "no Bible, no breakfast!"). I experienced an insatiable hunger for spiritual truth, and as the weeks passed, I experienced a decline in my internal, gnawing hunger. The glamour subsided, however, when I was confronted with biblical standards about the role of women. As with Eve in the Garden of Eden, Satan tried his lies on me, saying, in essence: "Surely your *loving* heavenly Father did not mean that you, an educated woman, would be subjected to those archaic standards!" (Genesis 3:1–7). By God's grace, I did not linger to discuss the matter with Satan but rather continued to "grow in the grace and knowledge of our Lord and Savior Jesus Christ" (2 Peter 3:18). As a result of my growth I have learned:

- *My heavenly Father does not offer a "cafeteria plan" for obedience* (James 2:8–13). We live in a world that promotes, "have things your own way." I learned that to please my heavenly Father I needed to respond to all of His instructions with an obedient spirit (1 Samuel 15:22; Psalm 51:16–17). I am not to merely pick and choose those that appeal to me. I also learned that asking forgiveness rather than permission was an unacceptable behavior (James 4:17).
- *God's Word is true whether or not I choose to embrace its teaching* (Hebrews 4:12–13). I began to mature spiritually at a time when miniskirts were the rage—and though my skirts were not as short as some others, they were definitely shorter than what belonged on a woman desiring to reflect godly character. It seemed that every time my roommate and I attended a worship service, Pastor LaHaye somehow integrated skirt lengths into the sermon (his recurring statement went something like, "children used to hide behind their mother's skirts—now they can't reach them!"). Consequently, "roast pastor" was often a choice part of our Sunday lunch, and we frequently asked

one another, "What is *his* problem?" Again, however, as we studied the Scriptures and desired to respond in obedience to them, we found that we chose to lengthen our skirts (1 Timothy 2:9; 1 Peter 3:1–6). It was not long until we realized that the problem was not Pastor LaHaye's, but ours.

- *My Creator has no obligation to explain His reasoning to me* (Isaiah 45:9; Romans 11:33–36). I learned a valuable lesson from my parents that helped immensely in my spiritual growth. As a child I often lacked the maturity to understand the reasons that motivated their decisions. However, as I matured, I understood why they insisted that I follow their instructions or why their answer was sometimes "no" to my heartfelt pleas. My father seldom changed his reasoning. And as I matured, I saw that he had proved himself credible over the years. The same thing is true in our relationship with our heavenly Father. At times we make a judgment about the validity of His instructions before we have cultivated a trustworthy relationship with Him. Second Peter 3:18 encourages us to "grow in the grace and knowledge of our Lord and Savior Jesus Christ," and as we do, the more His character will be reflected in our lives and the less concerned we will be about understanding all of the "whys."

- *I must exercise faith to embrace teaching that is contrary to cultural trends* (Hebrews 11:6). When God's instructions deviate from what society says will make me happy, I am to trust that "no good thing does He withhold from those who walk uprightly" (Psalm 84:11). My only responsibility is to make sure that I am choosing to walk uprightly—and that is an act of the will, not the emotions.

THE WISE WOMAN UNDERSTANDS GENDER EQUITY FROM A BIBLICAL PERSPECTIVE

He created them male and female,
and He blessed them and named them man
in the day when they were created.

GENESIS 5:2

The politics of race, gender, sexual orientation, socioeconomic class, age, religious belief, and disability dominated the culture of the nineties. Clustered under the umbrella of diversity, writings on these differences have impacted every dimension of society. These writings are found in many mediums—from scholarly publications to newspaper articles. Within the academic arena, one regional accreditation agency's *Handbook of Accreditation* moved from having a one-sentence footnote about diversity in its 1982 edition to an eight-page appendix on this topic in its 1997 Supplement to the January 1988 edition.[4] Similarly, the California Commission for Teacher Credentialing,[5] the agency controlling whether or not a college or university may issue teaching credentials, requires that programs explain how they dedicate time to instructing future teachers about diversity and equity during their application process. Failure to comply with the diversity guidelines from either of these agencies places the institution's ability to grant accredited degrees and teaching credentials in jeopardy.

The role of women and girls in education and the work force began to change significantly with the passage of Title VII and Title IX as a part of the Education Amendments to the Civil Rights Act of 1964. Title VII is the backbone of federal anti-discrimination legislation, while Title IX ensures legal protection against discrimination for students and employees. Title IX laid the foundation for much of the Affirmative Action legislation. The implications of this legislation have impacted the

Christian community. Let's take a look at some biblical principles that will help us formulate a Wise Woman's philosophy of gender equity.

PRINCIPLE ONE: GENDER EQUITY WAS ESTABLISHED IN GENESIS

The account of the creation of man and woman in Genesis 1:27–28 reports that God created both man and woman in His image. Together they were to have dominion over the creation.

Both the Old and New Testament describe many examples of equality of the sexes in spiritual life and blessing:

- Deuteronomy 6:6–7 teaches that both men and women are responsible to teach their children to obey God's law and love Him.
- Proverbs 6:20 assumes that both sexes were responsible to teach the law of God to their children.
- In Exodus 20 the Ten Commandments were given to men and women.
- Exodus 12 describes the participation of men and women in one of the greatest celebrations of the Jewish calendar, the Passover.
- The angel of the Lord appeared to Hagar (Genesis 16:7–13) and the mother of Samson (Judges 13:3–5).
- From Deuteronomy 12:10–12, 1 Samuel 1, and 2 Samuel 6 we learn that women shared in the great national celebrations of Israel.
- Nehemiah 7:67 reports a choir made up of 245 singing men and women that led the people to praise God through music.
- Exodus 38:8 relates that women served at the door of the tabernacle.

- Paul teaches in Galatians 3:28, "There is neither Jew nor Greek, there is neither slave nor free man, there is neither male nor female; for you are all one in Christ Jesus."
- Many New Testament teachings describe the high value that Jesus placed on women:

  a. John 4:1–26 records that He first revealed He was the Messiah to a woman.
  b. Jesus healed women (Matthew 8:14–15) and taught them (Luke 10:38–42).
  c. It was the women who remained at the cross after the men fled (Matthew 27:55–56).
  d. A woman was one of the first individuals to see the resurrected Christ (Mark 16:9; John 20:11–18).

- Paul honors women who serve faithfully in Romans 16 in the following ways:

  a. praising Phoebe as "a helper of many, and of myself as well" (Romans 16:1–2).
  b. commending Priscilla and her husband Aquila, "who for my life risked their own necks" for his sake (Romans 16:3–4).
  c. affirming Tryphena and Tryphosa, "workers in the Lord," and Persis "who has worked hard in the Lord" (Romans 16:12).

PRINCIPLE TWO: SCRIPTURE OUTLINES SPECIFIC ROLES FOR THE MALE AND FEMALE

Role differentiation is traced back to the lifestyle in Eden before sin impacted relationships (Genesis 2:7–23). Created by God, the specific roles for male and female were corrupted, not created, by the Fall. Genesis 1:26–28 directs man to have dominion not only over all animals but also over the earth from which he had been formed. God describes to Adam in Genesis 2:15–17 his specific duty of caring for his garden home. Even in a perfect environment, work was necessary for man's good, as well as his responsibility in bearing his Father's image. Genesis 2:18 (NKJV) reports God's final act of creation—the woman, to be a "helper comparable to him" (literally, "a helper like man"). As John MacArthur describes:

> When God saw His creation as very good (Genesis 1:31), He viewed it as being, to that point, the perfect outcome to His creative plan. However, in observing man's state as not good, He was commenting on his incompleteness before the end of the sixth day because the woman, Adam's counterpart, had not yet been created. The words of this verse emphasize man's need for a companion, a helper, and an equal. He was incomplete without someone to complement him in fulfilling the task of filling, multiplying, and taking dominion over the earth. This points to Adam's inadequacy, not Eve's insufficiency (cf. 1 Corinthians 11:9). Woman was made by God to meet man's deficiency (cf. 1 Timothy 2:14).[6]

Henry Morris (1976) describes this role differentiation by writing:

> Eve was thus made from Adam's side, to work alongside him in carrying out the divine commission to "fill the earth" and to "subdue" it. She not only had the same "flesh" (that is, *body*) and "life" (that is, *soul*) as did Adam, but she also had an eternal spirit, as he did; but the *spirit* (or, better, the "image of God") was directly from God, not mediated through Adam as was her physical life. This we know from Genesis 1:27: "So God created man in his own image . . . male and female he *created* them." The "image of God," directly created by God, was given to both man and woman. As "joined unto the Lord," however, even in this

dimension of life, they would become "one spirit" (1 Corinthians 6:17).[8]

First Corinthians 11:3–16; Ephesians 5:21–33; and 1 Timothy 2:11–14 charge man with a unique leadership role; this role is based on the permanent facts of creation, not temporary societal norms. In these verses we also find comparison of the roles of the Father and Son, which are different without inequity. The Greek word for *equal* defines things that are exactly the same in size, quality, character, and number. In every sense, Jesus is equal to the Father though Their roles differ (John 5:17–47; 10:33, 38; 14:9; Philippians 2:5–8; and Hebrews 1:1–3).

Genesis 3:16, Proverbs 31:10–31, Ephesians 5:22–33, Colossians 3:18–22, and 1 Peter 3:1–7 clearly outline role distinction in the home. First Timothy 2:8–15 describes the role of men and women in the church, while 1 Timothy 3:1–7 outlines the qualifications for overseers (bishops, elders, and pastors) and 1 Timothy 3:8–15 states the requirements for deacons.

PRINCIPLE THREE: SPIRITUAL GIFTS ARE AVAILABLE TO BOTH GENDERS

The Bible teaches that each Christian is given spiritual gifts. These allow the church to function effectively (Romans 12:3–13; 1 Corinthians 12:4–30; and Ephesians 4:1–13). Spiritual gifts are not gender defined.

PRINCIPLE FOUR: THE CHRISTIAN IS TO WALK WISELY AND KNOW THE WILL OF GOD WHEN SEEKING EMPLOYMENT

Employment is one arena where gender equity is most frequently debated. Studies reveal that women typically earn three-fourths of the wages that men receive for the same work despite the passage of Title IX as a part of the Education Amendments to the Civil Rights Act of 1964. Equality under the law is supposed to make us gender blind in the workplace; however, application of the law is not always perfect. Because running into some kinds of challenges in the workplace is inevitable, it is important that the Christian seek God's will when pursuing employment so we can be confident in our callings and respond to difficulties with godly wisdom. Psalm 37:4 teaches, "Delight yourself in the Lord; and He will give you the desires of your heart," while Ephesians 5:17 instructs Christians, "Do not be foolish, but understand what the will of the Lord is." Once employed, Christians have a responsibility to pray for their employers (or masters, like Abraham's servant did in Genesis 24:12), obey them, (Ephesians 6:5), please them in all things that do not compromise biblical standards (Titus 2:9), and be content in their situations (1 Corinthians 7:20–21).

PRINCIPLE FIVE: THE CHRISTIAN COMMUNITY IS TO RESPECT THE AREAS WHERE SCRIPTURE IS SILENT ON GENDER ISSUES

Romans 12:4–5 and 1 Corinthians 12 clearly describe the gifts God gives to Christians—they are to be used faithfully to further His kingdom. Scripture outlines the roles of men and women (Genesis 2:7–23; 1 Corinthians 11:3–16; Ephesians 5:21–33; and 1 Timothy 2:11–14). Within the framework of the defined roles, diversity is allowed (Romans 12:4–5; 1 Corinthians 12). Physically and spiritually, men and women are far more alike than different (Genesis 1:26–28). Apart from their interdependence, neither could exist (Genesis 1:28). Together, in masculine and feminine distinction, they reflect the likeness of God (Colossians 3:8–11). In Christ, they are equally loved and accepted by God (Jeremiah 31:3, John 3:16), equally baptized into the body of Christ (Ephesians 4:4–6), and equally accountable to honor and love one another (Romans 12:9–10). Together they are called to ministry—to serve God and to serve one another in the attitude of Christ (Philippians 2:5–8). Where Scripture is silent on gender issues, it is a biblical response for the Christian community to affirm the divinely provided diversity rather than to create unnecessary gender boundaries (Philippians 2:14–16).

I have spent the majority of my professional career in Christian higher education. At the same time, I have maintained memberships with professional organizations, as well as contacts with other Home Economics educators. When I attend meetings, the topics eventually move to the challenges that are a part of the profession. As my professional counterparts discuss areas of concern, they eventually speak to me with compassion—"If we have the challenges with *our leadership,* we can't imagine what you must have to deal with in a *faith-based institution!*" I am always pleased to respond that I am neither a "token woman" nor an "invisible woman" in my professional environment. As a matter of fact, my leadership has always encouraged me to reach my full spiritual and professional potential. When the *MacArthur Study Bible* was first released, Dr. MacArthur gave each Master's College faculty member a copy. I am encouraged each time I open the cover and read his inscription to me, "To Pat in gratitude for your exemplary leadership."

A FINAL THOUGHT . . .

Two women emerged on the political scene during my adult years, both professing to speak for the women of America— Betty Friedan founded the National Organization for Women (NOW) while Beverly LaHaye established Concerned Women for American (CWA). Betty built her platform on the societal trends of the day, while Beverly's was founded on the changeless character of God (James 1:17). NOW members of the twenty-first century are dissenting as a new generation of members embraces attitudes that their founders rejected.[8] CWA is the nation's largest public policy women's organization, with a membership of over half a million. Maintaining their original mission to promote biblical values among all citizens, they continue to speak for true womanhood.[9] As you ponder your long-term impact on others, consider these questions:

- Who am I most like, Betty or Beverly?
- Am I embracing the societal trends of the day or the changeless character of God?

GROWING IN UNDERSTANDING AND APPLYING GOD'S SPECIAL INSTRUCTIONS TO WOMEN

1. Search each of the verses listed in the "The Wise Woman Searches for God's Special Instructions to Women" section. Read them in the context of the Bible chapter in which they were written. Personalize your search by completing the chart below.

GOD'S SPECIAL INSTRUCTIONS TO [*YOUR NAME*] A WISE WOMAN IN PROGRESS		
Verse(s)	Instruction	Personal Application
Genesis 1:27	Aware that she was made by God in His own image	
Genesis 2:18, 21–24	A companion, helper, and an equal to her husband	
Proverbs 11:16	Gracious	
Proverbs 11:22	Discreet	
Proverbs 12:4	The crown of her husband	
Proverbs 14:1	Careful to build her house following the way of wisdom described in Proverbs 9:1–6, Proverbs 14:1	

GOD'S SPECIAL INSTRUCTIONS TO [*YOUR NAME*] A WISE WOMAN IN PROGRESS		
Verse(s)	Instruction	Personal Application
Proverbs 18:22; 19:14	An asset to her husband	
Proverbs 19:13; 21:9, 19; 25:24; 27:15–16	The opposite of the contentious wife described throughout the book of Proverbs	
Ruth 3:11; Proverbs 31:10–31	Virtuous; Worthy of Praise	
Ecclesiastes 7:26–28	Cautious to not cultivate the behaviors of a seductress	
Isaiah 3:16–24	Guarded in her behavior so she does not gain the reputation of the daughters of Zion	
Ephesians 5:22–23	Submissive to her husband	
1 Timothy 2:9	Modest; her clothing reflecting that her heart is focused on God—especially for worship	
1 Timothy 2:10	Careful to develop a personal testimony consistent with her profession of faith	
1 Timothy 2:11	Teachable	
1 Timothy 3:11	Trustworthy in all aspects of her life and ministry	

GOD'S SPECIAL INSTRUCTIONS TO [YOUR NAME] A WISE WOMAN IN PROGRESS		
Verse(s)	Instruction	Personal Application
1 Timothy 5:1–16	Willing to help widows in need	
2 Timothy 1:5	Grounded in the Word of God	
Titus 2:3–5	Available to teach the younger women	
1 Peter 3:1–6	Excited about developing the type of character that pleases her heavenly Father	

2. *Study the lives of each of the women described in the poem, "Did They Know?" Purpose to learn from their examples by completing the following chart.*

GOD'S SPECIAL INSTRUCTIONS TO [YOUR NAME] A WISE WOMAN IN PROGRESS		
Woman	Scripture Reference	Personal Application
Sarah		
Rahab		
Ruth		
Naomi		
Esther		
Mary		
Anna		
Elizabeth		
Eunice		

3. Spend a month (select one with thirty-one days) study-ing the book of Proverbs.

- *Look for and record examples of both the Wise and Foolish Woman.[11]*
- *Describe how your behavior aligns with theirs.*
- *Set personal goals that will focus your behavior on becoming a Wise Woman.*
- *Share your goals with someone who will hold you accountable for integrating them into your life.*

4. Review the biblical principles about gender equity and the supporting Scriptures presented in this chapter. Using them as a foundation, develop your philosophy of gender equity.

5. Consider the questions posed at the conclusion of this chapter:

- *Who am I most like, Betty or Beverly?*
- *Am I embracing the cultural trends of the day or the changeless character of God?*
- *Using the Scriptures presented in this chapter, and supported by your own Scripture search, formulate a* Life Mission Statement *that reflects your understanding of God's Special Instruc-tions to Women. For example, my* Life Mission Statement *is to:*

  a. Love my Lord with all my heart (Mark 12:30).
  b. Walk worthy of my profession (Ephesians 4:1–3).
  c. Train the younger women (Titus 2:3–5).

I often have the opportunity to spend time with younger women. We usually do not have a formal agenda—they just come over to my house "to talk." Sometimes we will sit outside on the back patio and talk while we watch my children play. We talk about lots of different topics based on the questions the young women ask—how to organize meals, how to clean our homes, how to support our husbands, how to grow in character traits such as patience or joy, and the list goes on. We identify a few things we can work on and set some goals for the coming week. Our "talking" the following week begins by reviewing the progress we made toward our goals.

One question that has been repeatedly asked over the years by my young friends is about submission. They will often ask, "Is it hard to submit to your husband?" After giving this question some thought the first time I was asked, my honest answer was, "No, generally it is not hard to submit to my husband." Do I perfectly practice the principle of submission? No. Do I have differing opinions with my husband? Yes, sometimes. Do I always agree with my husband? I agree with him most of the time, but not always. Does my pride cause me to be unsubmissive? Yes, unfortunately, it does sometimes. But because I am confident submission is a blessing, not a curse, a protection, not a restrainer, I attempt to joyfully practice the principle of submission. When I do this, submission is not difficult.

Of course this is not "enough" of an answer to give young women searching for understanding, so I began to reflect on WHY submission is such a hard principle for many young women to embrace. I began to realize two important facts. First, women have been fed many lies in our culture, and as a result, even Christian women desiring to be godly struggle with a proper understanding of submission. Women do not have an accurate definition of biblical submission. The world belittles most forms of submission to authority. Many Christian women forget that submission is a requirement for all Christians—not just women. Women do have an added dimension to submission if they are married—they are called to additionally submit to their husbands. But submission is a spiritual issue, not a women's issue. Submission does not mean that I am inferior to my husband or men, weak in intelligence, or lacking in strength; submission means that I am being obedient to God and His Word.

Secondly, I realized that many women have not been given an accurate picture of how submission is "fleshed out" in a marriage relationship. They are fearful because the picture they have of submission is of a dictator, not a loving leader. This gives me an opportunity to share with my young friends what a blessing it is to be married to my husband. I have a godly husband who lovingly leads and gives a genuine picture of Christ's love for His church. He works hard to sacrificially love each member in our family. Because of his compassionate and gentle leadership in our home, submission is easy. I can trust that my husband will make decisions that are for my good and the good of our family. He is quick to seek my input because of his love and respect for me. He values my opinions. I share with young women that submission is an umbrella of protection for me as a woman, not a stifling rope around my neck. Submission is meant for my good. I have been married long enough to experience God's blessings in my life through the leadership of my husband—as I willingly submit. Numerous times I have followed the direction and counsel of my husband, and the Lord has richly blessed our family and me (including blessings I would not have experienced had I not been submissive). It is a joy to see how the Lord enriches your life as you practice the principle of submission. Biblical submission really works, ladies! I tell my young friends that . . .

THREE

THE WISE WOMAN EMBRACES SUBMISSION

But He gives a greater grace.
Therefore it says, "God is opposed to the proud,
but gives grace to the humble." Submit therefore to God.

JAMES 4:6–7

Submission is a topic that generates emotion and contro-versy. It is not a popular topic, especially among women who do not know the Lord or understand the true nature of bibli-cal submission. Many Christian women also struggle to en-thusiastically embrace the concept of submission. There are many questions that often arise when discussing submission. Why must I submit to authority? Does submitting mean I am inferior? Does submitting mean I will always agree with my au-thority? Does submitting mean I never voice my opinion? The questions could be endless. Scripture gives us clear principles regarding the nature of submission. These principles can be applied to questions regarding how women are to submit. The first place to start when discussing submission it to make sure we understand how Scripture defines submission.

THE PRINCIPLE OF SUBMISSION

Therefore humble yourselves under the mighty hand of God,
that He may exalt you at the proper time,
casting all your anxiety on Him, because He cares for you.
1 PETER 5:6–7

Submission is often identified as a "woman's issue" rather than a biblical issue. However, the principle of submission seen in Scripture is a requirement for *all* Christians. Submission from a biblical perspective can be defined as *accepting God-given authority.* Submission is practically applied when we willingly choose to place ourselves under the authority of another person. All Christians, male or female, are required to practice the principle of submission. Alexander Strauch suggests, "The word *submission* can hardly be used in our culture without misunderstanding and strong disdain. It is loaded with negative, provocative connotations, yet submission is a biblical word and a Christian virtue."[1]

The word *virtue* means it is a character trait, quality, or feature that should be seen in Christians. Virtues are those character traits that have merit or value. We who view submission as a *virtue,* view it as a positive character trait. This is in contrast to how the world views submission. As Christians, we need to move away from our "cultural" definitions of submission and look to the biblical definition of submission. Scripture identifies six broad categories within which we are called to submit to authority; they include:

1. GOVERNING AUTHORITIES

Romans 13:1–2 says, "Every person is to be in subjection to the governing authorities. For there is no authority except from God, and those which exist are established by God. Therefore whoever resists authority has opposed the ordinance of God; and they who have opposed will receive condemnation upon themselves." Scripture is clear that we are to respect our governing authorities. We may not always agree with every policy or procedure, but we are called to be submissive unless they require us to be disobedient to God's Word (see Acts 4:19–20; 5:28–29; 1 Timothy 2:1–2; Titus 3:1; and 1 Peter 2:13–17). We apply this type of submission by complying with laws and regulations; for example, obeying driving laws and paying taxes. There is no government on earth, good or bad, which has been established without the consent of God Himself (Psalm 62:11; 103:19; 1 Timothy 6:15).

2. MASTERS

First Timothy 6:1–2 says, "All who are under the yoke as slaves are to regard their own masters as worthy of all honor so that the name of God and our doctrine may not be spoken against. Those who have believers as their masters must not be disrespectful to them because they are brethren, but must serve them all the more, because those who partake of the benefit are believers and beloved. Teach and preach these principles." This admonition in Scripture was calling slaves to be submissive to their masters. "The term 'obedient' refers to continuous, uninterrupted submission to one's earthly master or employer, the only exception being in regard to a command that involves clear disobedience of God's Word (as illustrated in Acts 4:19–20)."[2] While we are not slaves in our society and our work conditions are very different from that of a slave (for example, we have the freedom to leave our jobs, a slave did not), a prudent application of this principle of submission is to the employer/employee relationship. Believers are called to be faithful employees who treat their employers with respect (see also Ephesians 6:5–6; Colossians 3:22; 1 Timothy 6:1–2; Titus 2:9–10; 1 Peter 2:18–20). We ought to be model employees who demonstrate reliability and give our best on every project or assignment (working as "for the Lord" as described in Colossians 3:23–24).

3. CHURCH LEADERSHIP/ELDERS

First Peter 5:5 (NKJV) states, "Likewise you younger people, submit yourselves to your elders. Yes, all of you be submissive to one another, and be clothed with humility, for 'God resists the proud, but gives grace to the humble.'" The term for "elders" used here refers to pastors or spiritual leaders of the church (see 1 Timothy 3:1–7 and Titus 1:5–9 for a description of the qualifications of elders).[3] Christians, as church members, are called to submit to the authority of the church. Younger believers are given an extra exhortation to treat those in spiritual leadership over them with respect and honor. An important lesson to remember here is that submission to authority is a sign of spiritual maturity (see also 1 Corinthians 16:15; 1 Thessalonians 5:12–14). *Mature believers submit to authority; immature believers do not submit to authority.* Christians are to be "clothed in humility" and should not view themselves as better than others or be too proud to serve (Psalm 138:6; Philippians 2:3–4; James 4:6).

4. HUSBANDS

Ephesians 5:22 says, "Wives, be subject to your own husbands, as to the Lord." Married women have an added dimension to submission. They are called to be submissive to their husbands. God has ordained, or divinely appointed, that husbands function as the head of the wife, just as Christ is the head of the church (Ephesians 5:23–25). The husbands are the authority within the marriage relationship and home. God knew the home would need leadership and structure with two sinful people living together under one roof. He clearly identifies what that structure should look like. A married woman is called to *willingly* submit to her husband (husbands are not called to demand submission). She submits because God has commanded it, and she desires to be obedient as a Christian. She submits in obedience just as fellow believers submit to other forms of authority—government, church, employers, or one another. Wives are to submit to *their own husbands,* not all men (see also Colossians 3:18–21 and 1 Peter 3:1–6). As the wife submits to her husband and the husband sacrificially loves his wife, they become a clear model of the relationship between Christ and His church.

5. PARENTS

Ephesians 6:1–3 says, "Children, obey your parents in the Lord, for this is right. Honor your father and mother (which is the first commandment with a promise), so that it may be well with you, and that you may live long on the earth." Scripture calls children to submit to the authority of their parents (Exodus 20:12; Deuteronomy 5:16; Proverbs 1:8), which, in turns means that they are obeying the Lord, Himself. Colossians 3:20 tells us that this obedience to parents pleases God.

6. ONE ANOTHER

Ephesians 5:21 (NKJV) says, "Submitting to one another in the fear of God." This passage is often used to teach "equal submission" or "mutual submission" between husbands and wives. It is also used at times to suggest that we are called to submit to everyone. However, if we place the verse in its proper context, we see that Paul is *not* teaching equal or mutual submission among marriage partners or everyone. He explains in the verses that follow that "submitting to one another in the fear of God" is primarily in the context of submitting to authorities in three relationships—wife to husband, slave to master, and children to parents (Ephesians 5:22–6:9). Alexander Strauch explains this passage by stating:

> Some commentators insist that Ephesians 5 teaches "mutual submission" between husband and wife. They cite Ephesians 5:21, "and be subject (*hypotasso*) to one another in the fear of Christ," and conclude that the husband should submit to the wife in the same way that the wife should submit to the husband. This interpretation of Ephesians 5:21 is incorrect. One cannot use verse 21 to sweep away the plain teaching of verses 22–23. What is meant by "be subject to one another" is explained in specific detail in the verses that follow. The specifics include wives being subject to their husbands. Of course, there is a sense in which the husband as a godly leader defers to his wife's counsel, correction, or request. True love submits and even sacrifices itself for the benefit of another (see 1 Corinthians 7:3–5). But the sacrifices of Christlike love do not eliminate the headship-submission structure of the marriage. The husband still retains an authority the wife does not have, and authority to which a godly wife willingly submits.[4]

It is clear as we look at this passage that husbands are not called to submit to their wives in the same manner (just as parents do not submit to children and slaves do not submit to masters). Likewise, Paul is not suggesting "mutual submission" but rather a "one-directional submission to authority."[5] Therefore, we cannot apply this passage to the concept of mutual submission. While it is not mandated for Christians to submit to "all other people," they may choose to submit to another person out of love, humility, and a desire to esteem the other person (Galatians 5:22–25; Ephesians 5:1–10). Believers are called to demonstrate humility and graciousness when they interact with fellow Christians (Philippians 2:1–11). Since believers are one with Christ, we are also one with each other (Galatians 3:28). We are to esteem others as better than ourselves and look out for the interests and needs of others over our own (Philippians 2:3–4). There is no place for spiritual pride. Therefore, we ought to be known by the compassion and care we demonstrate for one another (including meeting physical needs and spiritual needs).

THE ACTION OF SUBMISSION

Though the LORD is on high, Yet He regards the lowly;
But the proud He knows from afar.
PSALM 138:6 (NKJV)

Understanding whom we are to submit to is important because it removes the temptation for us (especially as women) to respond to authority based on *emotions*—meaning, if I "feel" like submitting I will or if I "feel" like you deserve to be submitted to, I will submit. Scripture *commands* us as Christians to submit to the authorities in our lives, regardless of how we feel. Many people determine a willingness to submit based on their feelings regarding respect or agreement with the person in leadership. But submission is not based on these two criteria—respect and agreement. How then do we practically "live out" submission? If we are accepting God-given authority in our lives, it will be evident in how we respond to those in leadership over us. The action of submission can be defined as:

- yielding to the action, control, or authority of another person;
- deferring to another's judgment or decisions;
- surrendering my will to another.

Submission is an *act of my will*. I choose to submit. I am not submitting because I am overcome with another's power or authority—I submit because I *willingly* acknowledge and defer to another's authority. Because of this, my submission communicates respect and honor to those I submit to. My husband often defines submission as "strength placed under authority." It takes a very mature person to willingly submit to authority.

THE OBSTACLES TO SUBMISSION

Whoever secretly slanders his neighbor,
him will I destroy;
No one who has a haughty look
and an arrogant heart will I endure.
PSALM 101:5

Why is submission such a hard principle to practice? While there may be many reasons, I have found in my own life that there are generally three things I am "lacking in" when I do not submit—a lack of humility, a lack of understanding, or a lack of faith. Let's examine these three areas as they relate to submission.

1. A LACK OF HUMILITY

I know in my own life that pride rears its ugly head quite frequently! Pride or arrogance is often the reason why we do not submit to authority. For example, pride says:

- I can make a better decision.
- I want to be in control.

- I demand or desire to be treated differently.
- I have rights.

Scripture calls a "haughty look [and] a proud heart" sin (Proverbs 21:4 NKJV). *Haughty* is a word we don't use everyday, but it means arrogant, conceited, or overconfident. Scripture says that everyone with a proud heart is an abomination, or a disgrace, to the Lord (Proverbs 16:5). It is clear that God hates pride (Psalm 101:5; Proverbs 6:16–19; 8:12–13). The reason God despises this is that a proud heart reveals that I am not seeking after God; in other words, I am choosing to live independently from Him (Psalm 10:4; 14:1). Scripture says that because of this independence proud people are often insensitive to their own sin (Psalm 36:1–2). A lack of submission to earthly authorities is often an indicator of the heart—a heart that is also not submitting to God's authority. I would encourage you to evaluate if pride is a reason that submission is a difficult principle for you to embrace.

2. A LACK OF UNDERSTANDING

While ignorance is never an excuse to practice error, oftentimes we do not submit because we have not taken the time to study God's Word well enough to understand His commands and standards for our lives. Rather than thoroughly studying the Scriptures so we understand God's mind, we rely on the world's definition of *submission*. The world would have us believe that practicing the principle of submission is demeaning, humiliating, and shameful. Scripture says that submission is a means of demonstrating obedience and communicating honor to others. I would encourage you to evaluate what has influenced your view of submission. Is it the world's definition or is it God's Word? Do you view submission as being inferior or do you view submission as a Christian virtue?

3. A LACK OF FAITH

A third reason why we often do not practice the principle of submission is because we lack the faith or patience to see how God will provide for our needs and resolve an uncertain circumstance. I know in my own life that "doing nothing" is often the hardest thing to do. Rather than waiting on the Lord, as we are frequently admonished to do (for example, see Psalm 25:3–5; 27:14; 37:7–11), we desire to take matters into our own hands. We want answers to our questions, we want to have our plans made, and we want unknown circumstances resolved. But God is often calling us to wait and see how *He* will work in our lives. If we do not wait, we will rob ourselves of the blessing of seeing how God has worked in our lives. I was recently reminded of this truth while reading a book entitled *Biblical Womanhood in the Home*. One of the contributing authors, writing on the subject of submission, explains this principle as *allowing God to intervene*. What a great way to explain the idea of waiting on the Lord! She states:

> After Jesus died on the cross for our sins, God could have written in His Word, "If you confess with your mouth and believe in your heart that God raised him from the dead, you will be saved . . . The End." God could have left us here to deal with life and the devil on our own and just waited patiently until we died and went to heaven. The fact that He cares about every aspect of our lives between here and heaven is an incredible blessing. However, if we want to reap the reward, we have to allow Him to intervene. Remember: *Submission means God intervenes* . . . The last step is to *wait* on God to demonstrate what *His* will is concerning the situation. The goal is not to prove who is right and who is wrong, but to discover the will of God on the matter.[6]

I would encourage you to develop your faith so you are trusting in God and *His ability* to resolve circumstances in your life. Wait for God to intervene as you practice the principle of submission. The phrase *waiting for the Lord* in Scripture means that we are placing our "hope in" God or "expecting" the Lord to work His will in our lives. It suggests that we are patiently waiting and actively looking to His Word for courage, strength, and instruction about our life circumstances (Psalm 25:3–5; 27:14; 119:81; Isaiah 40:31). It means that we are submissive, patient, and confident because we have placed our hope in the Lord, even when the circumstances of our lives are not as we desire (Psalm 37:7; 40:1; 62:5; Romans 8:19–25). We are actively hoping in the Lord (Psalm 119).

MAKING A GODLY APPEAL TO AUTHORITY

The wise in heart will be called understanding,
And sweetness of speech increases persuasiveness.
PROVERBS 16:21

Understanding that we often lack humility, understanding, and faith will help us to practice the principle of submission. However, embracing these three concepts does *not* mean that we never offer an opinion, give advice, or make helpful suggestions regarding decisions or life circumstances. There are many times when is it appropriate—in the right manner and with a humble attitude—to offer counsel, make an observation, or offer support through words of encouragement to those in authority over us (for example, to our husbands or employers). It is during these times that a wise woman will understand how to "make a godly appeal." *Godly* implies that I am communicating in a biblical manner to those in authority over me (Ephesians 4:29–5:3; Colossians 3:8), while *appealing* means I am requesting that my authority reconsider or review a decision, instruction, or rule given to me. Making a godly appeal means

I am practicing submission even when I am offering counsel, communicating a personal opinion, or confronting a sin issue. Martha Peace describes a godly appeal as:

> Just because a woman is to be submissive does not mean that she should not have an opinion or request that her husband change his mind. If she desires to appeal one of his decisions (in a case where he is not asking her to sin), she should begin with something like "Would you consider . . ."

> Her husband would then realize right away that she is not demanding her way, but nicely making a request. She should end her appeal with something like ". . . but whatever you decide, I will do." Then she should *do* whatever he decides with a cheerful attitude realizing that it is the Lord Jesus she is ultimately serving. Her husband's answer (unless he is asking her to sin) is God's will for her at that time.[7]

Developing the habit of making a godly appeal will help us to practice submission even when our opinions differ from those in authority over us. I am often reminded of the verses found in Proverbs 15:1–2 (NKJV), "A soft answer turns away wrath, but a harsh word stirs up anger. The tongue of the wise uses knowledge rightly, but the mouth of fools pours forth foolishness." Here are a few practical suggestions for implementing the principle of making a godly appeal:

1. CHOOSE TO COMMUNICATE WITH RESPECT

Communicating with respect means we esteem and honor the other person at all times. Respectful communication *does not* use sarcasm, hateful words, harsh tones, or false statements. Respectful communication illustrates that I have a high regard for the *position* of the person in authority (my husband, employer, or elder, etc.), and I am striving to maintain an attitude of humility, not thinking of myself better than the other person (Romans 12:10; Ephesians 5:33; Philippians 2:3; 1 Peter 3:2). I encourage you to think in advance of how you can approach those in authority over you in a respectful manner. For example, I appeal to my husband by saying, "May I make a suggestion?" or "May I make an appeal?" My husband then knows I have information or counsel to offer related to the situation or decision he is making. This helps him to recognize I have something to contribute and it helps me to maintain a respectful attitude. If we are married, it is our responsibility to be our husband's helper—in all matters. Our goal in making a godly appeal is not to "get our way," but rather to encourage, edify, and inform.

2. Choose to Communicate with Gentleness and Love

Gentleness implies interactions filled with kindness or tenderness, with words that are carefully chosen (Proverbs 31:26; Galatians 5:22–23; 2 Peter 1:7). Love is clearly outlined in 1 Corinthians 13. This passage can become a practical checklist for communication by turning each principle into an evaluation question. For example you can ask yourself, "Am I patient? Am I kind? Am I being selfish?" Loving submission is willing to defer to the other person's opinion. This is important to remember when we make an appeal because we must still be committed to submitting to our authority even when he or she does not follow our counsel or advice.

3. Choose to Communicate at an Appropriate Time

Failing to be sensitive to the timing of our communication often results in failing to convey our message properly or effectively. For example, raising an issue with my husband as he is leaving for work is not an appropriate time. I will be rushed in my communication, and he will be limited in his time to respond and give direction. Our goal when making an appeal is to practice Proverbs 25:11 which states, "Like apples of gold in settings of silver is a word spoken in right circumstances," and Proverbs 15:23 which says, "A man has joy in an apt answer, and how delightful is a timely word!"

THE RESULTS OF SUBMISSION

It is better to be humble in spirit with the lowly
Than to divide the spoil with the proud.
He who gives attention to the word shall find good,
And blessed is he who trusts in the Lord.
The wise in heart will be called understanding,
and sweetness of speech increases persuasiveness.
PROVERBS 16:19–21

Practicing submission requires that we are discerning, wise, and Spirit-filled, which means we cannot practice submission in our own strength (Proverbs 16:20–21; 28:26; Ephesians 5:15–21). I have discovered that as I daily seek to submit to God's will, I am also better prepared to submit to my earthly authorities. Practicing the principle of submission results in many blessings, and some of the tangible results that I have experienced include:

- a yielding of my rights to those in authority over me. This allows me to both act and grow in the character trait of humility (Proverbs 15:33; 18:12; 22:4).
- the ability to give honor, respect, and communicate appreciation to those in authority over me. This allows me to practice the principle of esteeming others as better than myself (Philippians 2:3; 1 Thessalonians 5:12–13).

- deferring to the opinions *and* decisions of those in authority over me. This allows me to grow in my trust in God as I wait in patience to see how God will protect and provide for me (Psalm 27:14; 37:7–11; Proverbs 20:22).
- joy in obedience to God's Word. This allows me to experience God's blessing and helps me to continue to mature in my faith (1 Timothy 6:11–12; 2 Peter 1:5–11).

SUBMISSION FOR WIVES

Wives, be subject to your own husbands, as to the Lord.
EPHESIANS 5:22

Wives have the unique responsibility to submit to their own husbands. Unfortunately many wives do not *joyfully* embrace this command. Many have been confused by the world's message of independence for women. What does submission practically look like for wives? Let's apply the principles of biblical submission to the role of being a wife:

TO **WHOM** DO I SUBMIT?

Wives are called to submit to *their own husbands* (Ephesians 5:22; Colossians 3:18; Titus 2:5). This is important to remember because, practically speaking, in the daily operations of home, work, raising your children, ministry obligations, and other decisions, only the opinion of your husband matters (as he follows God and His Word). Women are not called to submit to all men. Wives are called to submit to their own husbands. Women submit to other men and women when it is appropriate for all believers to submit to authority (e.g., employer, church leadership, elders, or when esteeming others).

HOW DO I SUBMIT?

I have found the following three principles helpful in "how" I should submit:

1. I FOCUS ON MY RESPONSIBILITY.

This prevents me from becoming a nagging, unhappy, discontented wife. As I choose to do what is right before the Lord, I am focused on what He has called *me* to do. This prevents me from stewing in bitterness over difficult life circumstances or evaluating how well I think my husband is doing in leadership—neither of which matters! I am called to submit and trust the Lord to provide for my needs and lead through my husband. Instead of trying to take control of the situation I ought to pray that God works in my husband's heart and through his leadership. I am free to make godly appeals, when appropriate, as we discussed earlier.

2. I FOCUS ON SUBMITTING "AS TO THE LORD" (EPHESIANS 5:22)

I submit to my husband *because* I desire to please God by being obedient. My obedience brings Him glory (1 Corinthians 10:31). Since Scripture clearly states that submission is God's will for me, I bring Him glory when I choose to submit.

3. I PRAY FOR MY HUSBAND

I pray that he will be discerning, wise, and sensitive to the Lord's leading. I pray that I will be like-minded with my husband's decisions. I pray that I will give thoughtful and helpful input when my husband asks for my counsel. Prayer is the key to waiting and allowing God to intervene (1 Thessalonians 5:16–18; 2 Thessalonians 1:11–12).

WHEN DO I SUBMIT?

Scripture says wives are to submit "in everything" (Ephesians 5:24). In all areas of your family life, your household management, your relationships with people—in all things and in everything! There are three practical steps that have helped me learn to submit to my husband "in everything."

1. I NEED TO BE CAREFUL TO INVITE MY HUSBAND'S INPUT ON EVERY MATTER

In the early years of my marriage, I was surprised that my husband had opinions about things I thought were "my domain." For example, my husband enjoys decorating our home. I had to learn to work together with him in this area. I had to learn to seek his input and be willing to "submit" when his opinion differed from mine. Some of you may be thinking right now, "My husband couldn't care less what the color of the carpet is or what the window treatments look like!" If so, great, your husband has delegated this area to you. The main point here is that you do not assume that he does not have an opinion—your goal is to invite his input on every matter and create a home environment that is pleasing to him. While we are not to submit to husbands who are asking us to violate God's direct commands, we are called to seek to be submissive in all things. Nancy Wilson says:

> Of course some will immediately think of extreme cases where submission would be impossible. I am not talking about submitting to your husband if he tells you to violate God's express commands. I am talking about everyday submission. Submission means the act of yielding or surrendering, deferring, giving way. It is a positive thing, not a negative thing. We are to be obedient to our own husband as it says in Titus 2:5. This means in all things. Yes, regarding the household, the finances,

the children's discipline, education, and training, and so forth. What does your head think about these things? How does he want you to handle the situations that arise? Does he want you to ask your parents, in-laws, friends, or church elders before you ask him? We need to cultivate a high view of our husbands and a high view of their God-given jobs.[8]

Ladies, we are called to submit to our own husbands *in everything*. I would encourage you to develop the habit of seeking your husband's input. Here are some questions to help you begin thinking about this:

- What are his guidelines for disciplining and training your children?
- How would he like your household to be organized?
- How would he like your home to be decorated?
- What is his counsel regarding your commitments outside the home (e.g., ministry obligations, classes, or other regular commitments)?

2. I NEED TO RESPOND POSITIVELY RATHER THAN REACT TO MY HUSBAND'S LEADERSHIP

How easy it is for me to criticize and think of all the negative reasons why a decision my husband has made will "not work" for our family! Over the years, I have had to learn the habit of responding positively to my husband, particularly in the areas of travel and ministry opportunities. During our marriage my husband has suggested that we travel (and often move) to Mexico, New Zealand, Kazakstan, England, Israel, and make numerous trips across the United States! My first *reaction* is usually to think of our finances, our children's education, our health, leaving our family, or other challenges.

Fortunately, I have learned to *respond* positively, saying something like "Yes, OK, sounds interesting, let's talk about it!"

You see, my husband has a deep compassion for the lost world. He is much more of a visionary than I am, and if I did not respond positively over the years, I would have significantly impacted *and limited* his ministry. True, I still think about the challenges—but it does not have to be the first thing out of my mouth! By the way, during our marriage my husband has actually traveled everywhere that I mentioned earlier! And our family has accompanied him on several of the trips. He has had many opportunities to teach overseas and develop international ministries that I would never have dreamed of! Ladies, don't limit or discourage your husbands by your negative responses. I would encourage you to think about how you can respond positively, take time to pray through the decisions or opportunities that your husband presents, and then, at an appropriate time, give him your honest counsel; this will more likely be a thoughtful response rather than an emotional reaction.

3. I NEED TO COMMUNICATE MY SUPPORT FOR MY HUSBAND

We should be our husband's greatest cheerleader, confidante, and encourager. We should be quick to affirm him. God has delegated a great responsibility to our husbands—they are called to lead and love as Christ (Ephesians 5:25–29). We should take the time daily, weekly, and monthly to affirm his leadership in our lives and home. I would encourage you to identify specific character traits you are thankful for and then take the time to affirm him regularly. Ideas for ways you can affirm your husband include:

• Write him notes, letters, or cards affirming specific character attributes.

- Give him gifts representing your love and admiration for him (think of gifts that would have meaning to him—not you).
- Complete tasks or "do things" for your husband that communicate your love for him (e.g., running errands or completing household chores that are helpful to him).
- Listen to him. Yes, listening is a great gift to your husband and can be a tool for affirming him. Listen carefully so you learn your husband's heart. Give him your honest input after you understand his perspective.

WHY DO I SUBMIT?

At this point of our discussion, the reasons why we submit are probably already clear, but let's review. There are three primary reasons why I submit to my husband. First, and the most important, is so the Word of God will not be dishonored (1 Timothy 6:1; Titus 2:5). You see, if I am not submissive to my husband, I am an unclear and confusing example of how the church submits to Christ (Ephesians 5:22–30). My character is not consistent with my claim to be a Christian. One author puts it this way:

> This is the purpose of godly conduct—to eliminate any reproach on Scripture. For a person to be convinced God can save from sin, one needs to see someone who lives a holy life. When Christians claim to believe God's Word, but do not obey it, the Word is dishonored.[9]

The second reason why I submit is to give my husband respect and honor. There is no greater way a wife can communicate her support, love, and confidence in her husband than to submit to his leadership. Our husbands know our weaknesses! They know we do not "naturally" submit! However, as we submit to their leadership they see our commitment to be obedi-ent to God's Word, they see God's work in our hearts, and they see we have intentionally chosen to trust God and His Word. Our submission communicates honor and respect for our hus-band's God-given authority. Finally, as I submit I have the op-portunity to increase my faith in God's provision and ability to intervene in my life circumstances. I can think of numerous times in my married life when I chose to submit to my husband's leadership and have seen God work through it. Don't rob your-self of seeing God at work in your life, home, and husband by refusing to submit.

WHAT PREVENTS ME FROM SUBMITTING?

As we have previously discussed, we may lack humility, understanding, or faith. Additionally, wives often have not "trained" themselves to *respond* in a submissive manner to their husbands. I know in my own life it seems to be easy to *react* rather than *respond* to my husband. "Reacting" in my life is seen when I am quick to give my opinions, criticize a decision, or say a harsh word before I have thoughtfully and prayerfully responded to his leadership. Martha Peace explains it this way:

A WIFE SHOULD TRAIN HERSELF TO BE BIBLICALLY SUB-MISSIVE. The Greek word "train" in the Bible is *gymnazo* from which we get our English words gymnastics and gymnasium. *Gymnazo* implies doing something over and over until a person does it right. So, when you are not submissive in a godly way, you can train yourself biblically by thinking through what you should have thought and done instead of what you did. Next, ask God's forgiveness, then your husband's forgiveness. You might want to say something to the effect of, "When I said and did . . . I was not submissive to you. If I had this to do over again, this is how I would respond—(give details of what you should have done).

Will you forgive me?" This process takes work, but it will profit you not only in this life but the one to come. After all, practice does make perfect! Your motivation would be based on personal profit to you now as well as profit in eternity (see 2 Corinthians 5:10).[10]

I encourage you to "train" yourself to be submissive. Be quick to seek your husband's forgiveness when you have failed to respond appropriately.

WHERE DO I SUBMIT?

1. IN MY HEART—JOYFULLY

Joy is the attitude that measures my commitment to submission. Evaluating my joy allows me to determine whether or not I am submitting as "unto the Lord." I am reminded of the saying "I may be sitting down on the outside, but I am standing up on the inside!" Submitting with joy means we are sitting down on the inside and outside! Joy is an indicator of the depth of our commitment to submission. Are we committed in "head knowledge" only, or are we committed in our hearts also?

2. IN MY HOME—MODELING

Submission in the home is especially critical if we have children watching how we are responding to our husbands. Our children are learning to "submit to authority" by how we submit to our husbands (in addition to how we train them to submit to our authority as parents). Children learn that their fathers are worthy of respect by the way their mothers treat him, honor him, and submit as wives. I would encourage you to learn how to make an appropriate appeal when you have disagreements with your husband. Take time to pray and thoughtfully respond, rather than emotionally react to your husband in front of your children.

3. IN PUBLIC—RESPECTFULLY

We have an opportunity to practice submission in public by:

- Communicating with respect (examples include: not interrupting, not speaking for him, allowing him to respond for the family).
- Not speaking poorly of him (examples include: not criticizing him with your friends, not complaining about his leadership, not contradicting him in public).
- Disagreeing privately (examples include: resolving conflicts at home or choosing an appropriate time away from the children to discuss differences of opinion).

As we conclude our discussion on submission as it applies to wives, there is one final aspect of submission we need to address—the role of our husbands. We have focused on our responsibilities as wives; however, this is only half of the picture of Christ and His church. It is appropriate that we are reminded that our husbands have a more difficult role than we do—to love as Christ loves! It is his divine calling to lead, protect, and provide for his wife and family (Colossians 3:19; 1 Timothy 5:8; 1 Peter 3:7). By God's grace, Christian husbands are able to uniquely honor and love their wives by modeling Christ's love for His bride, the church. Because of this desire to love sacrificially, husbands may choose to practically demonstrate their love in a variety of ways; for example, stimulating her spiritual growth (teaching or admonishing), providing for her physical needs (food and shelter), or even helping around the house. John Piper and Wayne Grudem explain the husband's role of loving his wife:

If you are married, you love your wife the way Christ loved the church and gave himself for her; you be a humble, self-denying, upbuilding, happy spiritual leader; that you consistently grow in grace and knowledge so as never to quench the aspirations of your wife for spiritual advancement; that you cultivate tenderness and strength, a pattern of initiative and a listening ear; and that you accept the *responsibility* of provision and protection in the family, however you and your wife share the labor.[11]

Husbands who are believers are called to lead like Christ (Ephesians 5:25–33). This means he loves his wife sacrificially. He keeps the good of his wife in view when making decisions and leading his family (spiritually, emotionally, and physically). He models servant leadership. He practices the principle of giving "preference to one another" in his leadership (Romans 12:10). A husband's leadership should provide an environment that allows his wife to develop to her fullest in all areas because he (the husband) is a steward of her and her abilities. Piper and Grudem describe what this leadership ought *not* look like:

> Any kind of leadership that, in the name of Christlike headship, tends to foster in a wife personal immaturity or spiritual weakness or insecurity through excessive control, picky supervision, or oppressive domination has missed the point of the analogy in Ephesians 5. Christ does not create that kind of wife.[12]

Regardless of how much practical assistance the husband provides or how effective he is at demonstrating Christlike love, wives can carry out joyful and complete submission because they have placed their dependence in God alone and have confidence in God's ability to provide for their every need (Philippians 4:19).

Christian husbands are called to model sacrificial leadership. Christian wives are called to model joyful submission. Abuses of the principles of submission occur when *either* the husband or wife does not fully carry out his or her divine obligations. It is crucial that both partners work together in the calling to model Christ's love for His church. If they do not, something similar to the worldly stereotype of submission in effect happens, and a relationship can become abusive, degrading, and unloving. Submission does not mean that I am inferior to my husband, weak in intelligence, or lacking in strength; it means that I am being obedient to God and His Word.

A FINAL THOUGHT . . .

As I have had the opportunity to study and reflect on the principle of submission over the years, I have been encouraged by many others who said they had to *learn* to be submissive. This is an encouragement because it gives me hope that I can continue to grow in my ability to be the woman that God created me to be. Practicing submission ought to be a joyful pursuit of women who desire to please God. Elizabeth George provides us with a fitting word of encouragement and conclusion to our discussion of submission:

> Your Christian character becomes evident each and every time you choose from your heart to bend, to yield, to honor, to submit to your husband. Submission to your husband is one way that you, as a woman, after God's own heart, honor God. So won't you—as I did—transfer the idea of submission from the human realm into the heavenly? Look full into God's wonderful face and then submit to your husband as unto the Lord.
>
> And what if you have no husband? God gives each of us, His children, a multitude of opportunities every day to develop a heart that honors other people. Out of honor for God, you can give preference to other people in your life (Romans 12:10). Your dedication to honoring people honors God and brings beauty to your life that reflects your heart after God.[13]

GROWING IN
EMBRACING SUBMISSION

*1. Review the various types of "authorities" that God
places in people's lives, as outlined in the first part of this
chapter. Write down to whom you are called to submit
(e.g., employer's name, husband's name, pastor's name).
Commit to praying for the specific needs of these individuals. Pray also that your heart would joyfully submit to
their leadership in your life.*

*2. Submission is a spiritual issue that begins with our de-
sire to be obedient to God and His Word. Take time to
study the key passages on submission for yourself. The
chart below can help get you started!*

Scripture References	Principles Taught	Practical Application
Ephesians 5:22–33		
Colossians 3:18–19		
Romans 13:1–7		
Titus 2:3–5		
I Peter 3:1–4		
Ephesians 5:21		

*3. We all have sin issues in our lives that prevent us from
practicing perfect submission. Review the "obstacles" identified in this chapter and evaluate if they are hindering
your ability to joyfully practice submission. Ask yourself:*

- *Do I lack humility? Am I a proud person?*
- *Do I lack understanding? Do I need to study God's Word more intently?*
- *Do I lack faith? Do I need to grow in my confidence in God to provide for my needs?*
- *Do I need to learn how to submit? How can I practice submission?*

4. *Here are some suggestions for wives to "train" themselves to practice joyful submission to their husbands:*

- *Respond to your husband's leadership rather than reacting to it. Think about specific strategies you want to incorporate into your life to allow you to prayerfully and thoughtfully respond to your husband's leadership rather than emotionally reacting.*
- *Intentionally invite your husband's input on all matters so you are practicing the principle of "submitting in everything." Identify areas in which you can invite your husband's perspective.*

5. *Read more about it! Visit your local Christian bookstore to select a book that will stimulate you to continue to practice submission. References to the books cited in this chapter are located in the endnotes.*

*O*ur students are taught throughout their degree programs that they are to "walk worthy of their calling" regardless of where our Lord places them vocationally. Whether a profession in a high-profile corporate position or a stay-at-home mom (she's a professional, too—just think about how much it would cost to hire someone to complete her tasks!), they are Christians first and professionals second. The academic content and skills they learn are 100 percent marketable and 100 percent transferable when they establish homes of their own. Yet while the professional practices of a woman's skills and training are looked upon with esteem, a woman who applies the very same skills in the home is labeled as "just a housewife." However, an analysis of her daily activities as a homemaker finds her functioning as an authority in the fields of child development and human relations. She has continuing research in the laboratory and the field (she usually works through theories in her head and tests them inside and outside the walls of her home). Additionally, she is a nutritionist, a consumer advocate, a caterer, a financial analyst, an expert in clothing selection and care, as well as an interior designer. Though possessing incredible time management skills, she maintains 12- to 14-hour workdays. She finds that her job is more challenging than most "professional" careers, and her rewards are in satisfaction rather than money. Because she chooses to do all things for the glory of God . . .

FOUR

THE WISE WOMAN VISUALIZES HER PROFESSION AS A HIGH CALLING

Let the word of Christ richly dwell within you,
with all wisdom teaching and admonishing one another
with psalms and hymns and spiritual songs,
singing with thankfulness in your hearts to God.
Whatever you do in word or deed,
do all in the name of the Lord Jesus,
giving thanks through Him to God the Father.

COLOSSIANS 3:16–17

What is your profession? Do you view it as a high calling, or do you begin your description of who you are and what you do with "I am just a _____"? The word *profession* is defined as "following an occupation as a means of livelihood,"[1] while an *occupation* is "a person's usual or principle work, especially in earning a living."[2] Whether a stay-at-home mom or a corporate executive, God's Word challenges women to do their work with enthusiasm—as for Him, not simply to please others (Colossians 3:23). To view our professions in ways that are pleasing to God, we need to determine what His standards are. Since He is *excellence* personified, it follows that the Wise Woman's conduct will be one of *excellence*.

THE WISE WOMAN EMBRACES GOD'S ATTITUDE TOWARD EXCELLENCE

Praise the LORD in song,
for He has done excellent things;
Let this be known throughout the earth.
ISAIAH 12:5

God cares about excellence! Throughout the Scriptures we are reminded that Christians will be judged on the quality of their work (1 Corinthians 3:13, 4:5; 2 Corinthians 5:10; Revelation 20:12). Practically speaking, whether we are baking a pie or preparing a financial portfolio, our deepest motivation ought to be pursuing excellence.

1. Psalm 8:1 teaches us that God's name is excellent. Since we are His representatives, when people speak of us it should be in terms of excellence. Proverbs 22:1 reminds us, "a good name is to be more desired than great wealth."
2. Deuteronomy 32:1–4 describes God's work as being excellent. Likewise, the description of the Wise Woman of Proverbs 31:10–31 begins with the question, "An excellent wife, who can find?" The tone of the question suggests that such a woman does exist, but is very hard to find. As daughters of our heavenly Father, we will want to be numbered in this minority—though others may choose to "cut the corners" in their work, we will endeavor to put a signature of excellence on all that we do.
3. Second Samuel 22:31 depicts God's way as being excellent or blameless. Would others agree that we are people of *integrity?* Matthew 5:48 reminds us that we are to seek to be perfect as our heavenly Father is perfect.

4. Romans 12:2 challenges us to focus on the excellence of God's will. My dear friend and spiritual mentor Verna Birkey taught me that as God's dear child, nothing happens to me that has not already gone through His grid of approval. What is our response when something happens that we don't like? Do we still believe that God's will is excellent? Regardless of the circumstances, Romans 12:2 directs us to God's standard of holy living.

5. Psalm 36:7 portrays God's lovingkindness as being excellent. This lovingkindness is much like the protective care of a mother bird for her young. Do others find our actions toward them protective and nurturing or hostile and antagonistic?

6. Leviticus 1:10 and 22:19–25 report that the Old Testament sacrifices represented the best available to the worshiper. The offerings were to be the finest of the flock without defect. Within the sacrificial system, God required the best grain, the best fruit, and the best sheep. And God still wants the best His people can bring! So, when we clean our home, complete a project, or extend hospitality, are we giving our best, or is our "sacrifice" one that is brushed, crushed, torn, or cut? (Leviticus 22:24).

As Wise Women in progress let's ask ourselves some probing questions as we evaluate our attitude toward excellence.

DO I:

1. Pursue excellence?
2. Believe that I am fearfully and wonderfully made by God?
3. Strive for quality?
4. Believe I was created to excel, designed to achieve, and reborn to climb higher?

5. Keep focused that God is excellence personified and that as His daughter my behaviors should reflect Him?

6. Demonstrate excellence in my professional behavior by:

- the responsibility I exhibit? (Ephesians 6:5)
- persevering when quitting appears to be the logical choice? (Philippians 3:13)
- consistently working hard? (Colossians 3:23)
- demonstrating loyalty? (1 Corinthians 15:58; Galatians 6:2)
- projecting confidence? (Philippians 4:13)
- displaying graciousness? (Proverbs 11:16)
- rising above circumstances and choosing to manifest a joyful outlook toward life? (John 10:10)
- understanding that the fear of the Lord is the beginning of wisdom and that fools despise wisdom and instruction? (Proverbs 1:7)

Keep your answers to these questions in mind as we explore the characteristics of . . .

WALKING WORTHY OF OUR PROFESSIONS

Therefore I, the prisoner of the Lord,
implore you to walk in a manner worthy of the calling
with which you have been called,
with all humility and gentleness,
with patience, showing tolerance for one another in love,
being diligent to preserve the unity of the Spirit
in the bond of peace.
EPHESIANS 4:1–3

The apostle Paul opens the fourth chapter of Ephesians (NKJV) with the challenge, to "walk worthy of the calling with which you were called." Several words and phrases assist us in understanding Paul's instructions—*therefore, the prisoner of the Lord, walk worthy,* and *calling:*

> *Therefore* marks the transition from doctrine to duty, principle to practice, position to behavior. *The prisoner of the Lord*—by mentioning his imprisonment again, Paul gently reminded Ephesian believers that the faithful Christian walk can be costly and that he had paid a considerable personal price because of his obedience to the Lord. *Walk* is frequently used in the New Testament to refer to daily conduct, while *worthy* has the idea of living to match one's position in Christ. The apostle urged his readers to be everything the Lord desires and empowers them to be. *Calling* refers to God's sovereign call to salvation.[3]

Before we look at some specific qualities of the *worthy walk,* let's take a few moments for personal evaluation, beginning with the skills and abilities God bestowed upon you: Does your daily conduct reflect that you are a careful steward of them? What is your profession? Do you know its purpose and aims? Are you excited about the impact you that can make as a Christian? Very early in my Christian walk Verna taught me a motto that has consistently motivated my professional behavior: "I am a personal representative of the living God, on assignment to make God visible to others around me." As you function in your profession is your heavenly Father evident to those who interface with you?

QUALITIES OF THE WORTHY WALK

*For this reason also, since the day we heard of it,
we have not ceased to pray for you
and to ask that you may be filled with the knowledge of
His will in all spiritual wisdom and understanding,
so that you will walk in a manner worthy of the Lord,
to please Him in all respects,*

*bearing fruit in every good work and
increasing in the knowledge of God.*
COLOSSIANS 1:9–10

A variety of qualities will be evident in our lives if we are leading a life worthy of our divine calling, beginning with choosing to achieve at a level that fulfills God's summon to serve Him wholeheartedly. *Excellence* is the level we are to attempt to achieve as we serve our Lord in our professions as in the rest of our endeavors. We also have the privilege of being an example to others and therefore leading them closer to God. Regardless of our position, we must not demand that others reach a standard of performance that we are unwilling to embrace. Whether in the marketplace or the home, we are called to model the behaviors we expect others to practice. One of the greatest sources of accountability in my professional walk is my students. My office is close to their classrooms, and throughout the day they observe whether or not the character principles I teach them are important enough to me to implement them into my own life. They hear how I answer my phone, discern my attitude when I am interrupted, and observe how I interact with my faculty co-workers, administrative assistant, student worker, and guests to the department. Each moment I can either reinforce or negate my classroom instruction. Following the apostle Paul's instruction, I daily seek to live with humility, gentleness, and patience while I bear with others in love and maintain a unity of spirit.

Humility is the most foundational Christian virtue and is the quality of character commanded in the first beatitude, Matthew 5:3. Being *poor in spirit* (humble) is the opposite of self-sufficiency. This speaks of the deep humility of recognizing one's utter spiritual bankruptcy apart from God. It describes those who are acutely conscious of their own lostness and hopelessness apart from divine grace. *Gentleness* is an inevitable product of humility and refers to that which is mild-spirited and self-controlled, and *patience* means long-tempered and refers to a resolved patience that is an outgrowth of *humility* and *gentleness*.[4]

Bearing with others in love requires the application of *humility, gentleness,* and *patience*. The evidence of my application of this quality is demonstrated when I choose to maintain self-control when I am subjected to annoyance or provocation. It is my choice to continue to offer unconditional love even when others are acting in a way that would make it easy to withdraw my love. At times our Lord will place a student in our department who stretches my love; He has taught me to first examine the situation carefully. Am I irritated because I am seeing a mirror image of my behaviors and I don't like what I see? Or is God challenging me to practice the truth of 1 Peter 4:8 (NKJV), to "have fervent love for one another"? "*Fervent* means to be stretched or to be strained. It can be used to descrie a runner who is moving at maximum output with taut muscles straining and stretching to the limit. This kind of love requires the Christian to put another's spiritual good ahead of his own desires in spite of being treated unkindly, ungraciously, or even with hostility."[5]

As I choose to bear with others and make allowances for them rather than becoming annoyed or provoked, I am demonstrating my love for them, even when I don't love their behavior! Paul also reminds me that I am to eagerly and earnestly seek to "preserve the unity of the Spirit in the bond of peace" (Ephesians 4:3). Let's look at four keys to successfully practice the *worthy walk* Paul presents in Philippians 3:12–14.

KEYS TO THE WORTHY WALK

*Not that I have already obtained it
or have already become perfect,
but I press on so that*

I may lay hold of that for which
also I was laid hold of by Christ Jesus.
Brethren, I do not regard myself
as having laid hold of it yet; but one thing I do:
forgetting what lies behind and
reaching forward to what lies ahead,
I press on toward the goal for the prize
of the upward call of God in Christ Jesus.
PHILIPPIANS 3:12–14

The apostle Paul presents four keys to the *worthy walk* in Philippians 3:12–14 that provide direction to the twenty-first-century Wise Woman in progress—a genuine restlessness (Philippians 3:12), a solitary longing (Philippians 3:13), a wholehearted purpose (Philippians 3:12, 14), and a definite goal (Philippians 3:13, 14). Paul's *genuine restlessness* is a model for all believers; while he was satisfied with his Savior and his salvation, he was dissatisfied with his flesh. He was restless with his spiritual status because he was not all that he knew that he could or should be. "Paul uses the analogy of a runner to describe the Christian's spiritual growth. The believer has not reached his goal of Christlikeness, but like the runner in a race, he must continue to pursue it."[6] The Christian life is to be exciting—and as Wise Women we should be excited about growing, regardless of our spiritual age.

Paul's *solitary longing* helps us to eliminate the unnecessary from our lives. Our quest toward Christlikeness puts life into a single focus—Paul says this "*one* thing I do." As Wise Women we are to have only one goal—to serve God with our entire being (1 Corinthians 6:12). Our Lord Jesus serves as the ultimate role model for this solitary longing. "He did not finish all the urgent tasks in Palestine or all the things He would have liked to do, but He did finish the work God gave Him to do. The only alternative to frustration is to be sure that we are doing what God wants. Nothing substitutes for knowing that this day, this hour, in this place we are doing the will of the Father. Then and only then can we think of all the other unfinished tasks with equanimity and leave them with God."[7]

Paul's *wholehearted purpose* helped him to focus on his determination to keep moving toward the goal. We will not succeed if we do not have a strong determination, but its source must be executed in the strength of the Holy Spirit, not simply our sheer determination (Philippians 4:13). Are we mature enough to keep pursuing our "upward call" (Philippians 3:14) when it would be easier to quit?

Finally, Paul had a *definite goal,* and he moved toward it with tenacity. Serving God with our entire being challenges us to refuse to dwell on the past—regardless of whether it is filled with success or sin. What we are today is what counts! Paul challenges us to refuse to drink from the cup of self-pity and to release past grudges and incidents of mistreatment—he forgot these and climbed higher toward his goal! Now that we have established a biblical foundation for our worthy walk, it's time to identify some practical suggestions for implementing Christian integrity on the job:

- Learn the chain of command in your organization and focus on submitting to those in authority. Remember that submission is willingly placing oneself under someone else's direction. As employees we have a responsibility to respond positively to their leadership unless they ask us to fulfill a request that violates Scripture.
- Build an appropriate, positive relationship with your superiors. Look for ways to make them successful.
- Seek to establish positive relationships with co-workers. Romans 12:18 encourages us to do everything possible to work in harmony with others. Then if disharmony

surfaces, it will be the result of others' negative attitudes and responses, not yours.

- Study the politics of the organization, but stay away from involvement in organizational politics. If you are unavoidably drawn into a political situation, attempt to remain neutral.

- Refrain from criticizing the organization and the people in it. Choosing to think about what is good about it is a practical way to implement Philippians 4:8–9 into your daily life.

- Avoid becoming part of a clique, and as a new employee, don't team up with one person in the group too soon.

- Avoid being caught in the "everyone else is doing it" syndrome.

- Dress professionally, always giving priority to the principles of modesty presented in chapters nine and ten.

- Be a good steward of the organization's resources and display integrity when using them—for example, refrain from conducting personal business on company time and don't use company supplies for personal use.

- Grow graciously in your professional role. Proverbs 11:16 reminds us that "a gracious woman attains honor." This means not misusing others to achieve your goals and not flaunting your achievements. There is no advancement that is worth sacrificing your Christian reputation.

- Remember that you are the member of a team. Recalling the acrostic of the word TEAM—Together Everyone Achieves More—will help you focus on making your best contribution without trying to control every situation.

- Keep focused that the organization existed before you arrived and will more than likely survive after your departure. When you are in a position of leadership, make changes gradually—this strategy generally reduces animosity.

- Be the best employee you can be—purpose to function at a level of proficiency that reflects you are "walking worthy of your profession," practice flexibility, cultivate an attitude of contentment, solicit feedback from others, don't become defensive when others offer suggestions for improvement, be vulnerable, and always project a teachable spirit.[8]
- Share your faith by modeling it; communicate it on your own time, not your organization's time.
- Remember that your performance in this position is the foundation for God's next assignment for you. Make sure you are laying a solid foundation!

WHO IS YOUR ROLE MODEL?

Now these things happened to them as an example,
and they were written for our instruction.
1 CORINTHIANS 10:11

My ministry is grounded in learning from women of the Old and New Testaments. Early in my spiritual growth, I found that I could eliminate much spiritual and emotional turmoil in my life by examining the lives of the men and women written about in the pages of Scripture, learning from both their successes and failures (1 Corinthians 10:1–12). I carry this knowledge into the college classroom and assign my students studies of women of the Old and New Testaments each time I teach the class that includes the study of Proverbs 31:10–31. I remember well the young widow from Africa who came to the college to further her education. She was a relatively new Christian and had as her responsibility her young son and brother. After several weeks of classes she held up her textbook, and with tears in her eyes shared with the class, "This is my first Bible study book, and through it I have learned to read the Bible as a woman—I am beginning to understand that my heavenly Father loves women!" She summarized in those few words my passion for meeting the women of the Bible personally.

Three women who walk through the pages of Scripture provide us with role models for our journey of "walking worthy of our profession"—Mary, Martha, and Dorcas. Each offers positive and negative character qualities for us to emulate as we think of being a servant leader, the biblical approach to walking worthy of our profession (Mark 10:44–45). A servant leader models Mark 10:44–45 by becoming excited about making others successful—and that means she is more concerned about the achievements of others than her own advancement. This concept is beautifully captured in the classic children's story, *The Velveteen Rabbit:*

> The Skin Horse had lived longer in the nursery than any of the others. He was so old that his brown coat was bald in patches and showed the seams underneath, and most of the hairs in his tail had been pulled out to string bead necklaces. He was wise, for he had seen a long succession of mechanical toys arrive to boast and swagger, and by-and-by break their mainsprings and pass away, and he knew that they were only toys, and would never turn into anything else. For nursery magic is very strange and wonderful, and only those playthings that are old and wise and experienced like the Skin Horse understand all about it.
>
> "What is REAL?" asked the Rabbit one day, when they were lying side by side near the nursery fender, before Nana came to tidy the room. "Does it mean having things that buzz inside you and a stick-out handle?"
>
> "Real isn't how you are made," said the Skin Horse. "It's a thing that happens to you. When a child loves you for a long, long time, not just to play with, but REALLY loves you, then you become real."
>
> "Does it hurt?" asked the Rabbit.

"Sometimes," said the Skin Horse, for he was always truthful. "When you are Real you don't mind being hurt."

"Does it happen all at once, like being wound up," he asked, "or bit by bit?"

"It doesn't happen all at once," said the Skin Horse. "You become. It takes a long time. That's why it doesn't often happen to people who break easily, or have sharp edges, or who have to be carefully kept. Generally, by the time you are Real, most of your hair has been loved off, and your eyes drop out and you get loose in the joints and very shabby. But these things don't matter at all, because once you are Real you can't be ugly, except to people who don't understand."[9]

As you contemplate your profession, are you willing to allow our Lord to shape your character so that as you approach retirement age you are considered *real*?

Nine verses describe the three women who contribute to our composite role model; five are dedicated to Mary and Martha (Luke 10:38–42) and four to Dorcas (Acts 9:36–39). Mary's example teaches us our first priority as professional women—that of spending time with our Lord so that we are prepared to serve Him effectively. Luke 10:39 describes Mary as sitting at Jesus' feet and savoring His instructions. Mary sat long enough to listen to her Master before she performed a task that potentially had a long-term impact. Do our efforts produce short-term results or long-term impact? As I contemplate the response to this question I am reminded of Steve Green's song, "Find Us Faithful."[10] When my Lord calls me home or He comes for me, what evidence of my faith will others find when they sort through my belongings? Will they be drawn to the One who loved me and redeemed me or will they only be impressed by organizational and management skills? And when I meet my Lord, will He say of me, "Pat, you chose the good part, which will not be taken away from you" (Luke 10:42)? These questions motivate me to pray daily that I will choose to first embrace Mary's model.

Martha's word portrait reveals the second priority of walking worthy of our profession—learning to make good decisions. Martha was a woman who could think on her feet—notice that she was quick to extend hospitality to the Lord and His disciples. Luke 10:38 describes Martha as welcoming Him into her house—an admirable quality for all of us to emulate. However, Luke 10:40 suggests that though Martha had the right idea, the intensity of her approach to her responsibilities merited some softening. "Distracted literally means 'dragging all around'; the expression implies that Martha was in a tumult with much serving—that she was fussing about with details that were unnecessarily elaborate."[11] And what about the results of her fussing? She quickly developed a bad attitude toward Mary and was rebuked rather than affirmed by the One she wanted to please. We learn from Martha's life that she was successful in getting things done, making things happen, and clearly articulating her thoughts—all qualities that a successful professional woman desires. Blending Martha's efficiency attributes with Mary's tender spirit yields a powerful tool for our Lord's service—however it is only attainable as we allow Him to manage our lives.

The Valley of Vision: A Collection of Puritan Prayers and Devotions is a small book with a profound message. Its contents draw the reader back to "the largely forgotten deposit of Puritan spiritual exercises, meditations, and aspirations."[12] The following prayer, "Regeneration," reflects the influence that our Lord desires to have over the Martha portion of our character:

REGENERATION

O God of the highest heaven,

Occupy the throne of my heart,

take full possession and reign supreme,

lay low every rebel lust,

let no vile passion resist thy holy war;

manifest thy mighty power,

and make me thine for ever.

Thou art worthy to be

praised with my every breath,

loved with my every faculty of soul,

served with my every act of life.

Thou has loved me, espoused me, received me,

purchased, washed, favoured, clothed, adorned me,

when I was worthless, vile, soiled, polluted.

I was dead in iniquities,

having no eyes to see thee,

no ears to hear thee,

no taste to relish thy joys,

no intelligence to know thee;

But thy Spirit has quickened me,

has brought me into a new world as a

new creature,

has given me spiritual perception,

has opened to me thy Word as light, guide,

solace, joy.

Thy presence is to me a treasure of unending peace;

No provocation can part me from thy sympathy,

for thou has drawn me with cords of love,

and dost forgive me daily, hourly.

O help me then to walk worthy of thy love,

of my hopes, and my vocation.

Keep me, for I cannot keep myself;

Protect me that no evil befall me;

Let me lay aside every sin admired of many;

Help me to walk by thy side, lean on thy arm,

hold converse with thee,

That henceforth I may be salt of the earth

and a blessing to all.[13]

If you were asked who is managing the Martha portion of your character, what would be your response?

The brief description of Dorcas completes our composite role model portrait and provides our third priority—learning to be a disciple. When we hear the name Dorcas we conjure up pictures of the lady who was the seamstress of Joppa—but that's not how she is introduced. Acts 9:36 presents her as a disciple—the only woman in the Bible honored with that description. "*Disciple* means 'student,' one who is being taught by another."[14] Though we do not know who taught Dorcas, we do know that she possessed a teachable spirit because she was described as a disciple. We also know that she was "abounding with deeds of kindness, which she continually did." This would indicate that her teaching impacted her heart as well as her head and motivated kind actions, rather than simply making her arrogant. As we evaluate our professional experiences are we, as Wise Women, willing to learn from others? How does our accumulation of knowledge and training affect us—do we become arrogant, or does each phase of our professional development motivate us to greater acts of kindness?

Dorcas' life provides a final priority for us to weave into our composite role model—her willingness to use the skill she had to minister to the needs of others. Her profession, according to Acts 9:39, was that of seamstress, to a specific clientele—widows. Are we generous, wise stewards of the knowledge and skills that we have, or do we do one of the following: place a high price tag on them, minimize their importance, or "put it under a bushel"(Matthew 5:15)?

This chapter began with the focus that whether you are a stay-at-home mom or a corporate executive, God's Word challenges you to "walk worthy of your calling." The lives of Mary, Martha, and Dorcas challenge us to maintain four priorities:

1. spending time with our Lord so that we are prepared to serve Him effectively,
2. learning to make good decisions,
3. having a teachable spirit (becoming a disciple), and
4. possessing a willingness to use our skills to minister to the needs of others.

To be spiritually effective, these priorities need to be motivated by a heart of love rather than desires for self-fulfillment (Galatians 5:13). Often, however, the application of the principles begins with an act of the will—that is doing the right thing and then allowing our emotions to catch up with us (remember the book of Psalms is directed to our will, not our emotions). Combining biblical role models with the instruction of the Psalms, let's pursue our worthy walk while modeling the mind-set of other godly women.

⌒

I WILL, LIKE . . .

The Queen of Sheba, diligently seek godly wisdom (1 Kings 10:1–13);

Ruth, respond to the advice of older women (Ruth 3:1–6);

Sarah, submit to those in authority over me (1 Peter 3:6);

*The little Jewish maid, boldly, but appropriately, speak of my faith
(2 Kings 5:1–14);*

Esther, choose to take risks to further God's kingdom (Esther 4:1–17);

*The widow of Zarephath, trust my heavenly Father to multiply my
resources (1 Kings 17:10–24);*

The Shunammite woman, extend hospitality (2 Kings 4:8–37);

*Mary, the mother of Jesus, wholeheartedly declare myself a bondslave
of the Lord (Luke 1:26–38);*

*Elizabeth, believe that God works miracles in women of all ages (Luke
1:5–25);*

*Mary of Bethany, listen to my Master's words with a teachable spirit
(Luke 10:38–42);*

*The poor widow, give out of my need rather than my abundance
(Mark 12:42);*

Mary, exhibit humble love and devotion for my Lord (John 12:2–3);

*The woman with the lost coin, approach each responsibility with tenacity
(Luke 15:8–10);*

Dorcas, share my talents with those in need (Acts 9:36–41);

Lydia, choose to use my profession for God's glory (Acts 16:14, 40);

Lois and Eunice, endeavor to leave a godly heritage (2 Timothy 1:5);

*The Wise Woman of Proverbs, purpose to fear my Lord (Proverbs
31:10–31);*

*Realizing that I cannot hope to achieve these goals in my own strength
I will rely upon Him, for I can do all things through Christ who
strengthens me (Philippians 4:13).*

A FINAL THOUGHT . . .

If we are to visualize our profession as a high calling, we will choose to delight ourselves in the Lord (Psalm 37:4–5). This means that we will wholeheartedly serve our Lord at all times, in all places, and in all situations.

Lisa and I both pursued doctoral studies while we were employed full-time; that meant that we turned our attention to our academic studies after our preparation for our professional responsibilities were completed. A myriad of challenging situations befell each of us as we pursued our degrees. The final requirement for the degree was a dissertation—a lengthy research project. "Write, rewrite, and write again" was the motto of that phase of our studies, and at times we wondered whether we would ever see them in bound format—but by God's grace we finished. The tenacity required to complete the dissertation prepared us to meet the manuscript deadline for *Becoming a Woman Who Pleases God;* again, we both had full schedules— which meant our writing began after the responsibilities of the day were completed. We learned an entirely different application of the Virtuous Woman's "lamp not going out by night" (Proverbs 31:18) as the manuscript emerged! Had we stopped "reaching forward" with the dissertations, *Becoming a Woman Who Pleases God* would probably still be a dream.

The ink was scarcely dry on the approval page of Lisa's dissertation when she learned that she was expecting their first child. As I watched her change her professional suits for maternity clothes, I also observed that she moved into her new role with the same level of excellence that she had approached her teaching responsibilities and doctoral studies. Her faithfulness as a professional and a student prepared her for the Lord's next assignment—one she will share with you as she provides practical tips for new mothers in chapter five.

GROWING IN
VISUALIZING OUR
PROFESSION AS A
HIGH CALLING

1. *Read* Brokenness *by Nancy Leigh DeMoss.*[15] *Use the questions on page 149 to evaluate your status as either a proud person or a broken person.*

2. *Review the principles of submission presented in chapter three and develop strategies to relate them to your professional responsibilities.*

3. *The lives of Mary, Martha, and Dorcas challenge us to maintain four priorities:*

   - *spending time with our Lord so that we are prepared to serve Him effectively,*
   - *learning to make good decisions,*
   - *having a teachable spirit (becoming a disciple), and*
   - *possessing a willingness to use our skills to minister to the needs of others.*

Evaluate your life in relation to each of the priorities by completing a chart like the one on the next page:

Priority	My Definition of the Priority	Personal Goals I Will Set to Activate the Priority
Spending time with my Lord.		
Learning to make good decisions.		
Having a teachable spirit.		
Using my skills to minister to the needs of others.		

4. *Using the "I Will . . ." portion of this chapter as a model, write your commitment to walking worthy of your profession.*

- *Support each "I Will . . ." with Scripture.*
- *Ask someone to hold you accountable to fulfilling your commitment.*

*M*y husband and I were "older" first-time parents, which gave us a unique perspective on the privilege it is to become a parent. We do not take lightly the truths found in Psalm 127:3: "Behold, children are a gift of the Lord, the fruit of the womb is a reward." We understand the immense blessing and enormous responsibility it is to raise children. Throughout the many years that I waited to become a mother, God instilled in my heart the desire to pursue excellence in my role as a wife and, hopefully someday, as a mother. The Lord did eventually allow us to have two precious boys of our own.

However, the adjustment to motherhood was not an easy one for me. I experienced loneliness, confusion in my new role, and fatigue from physical exhaustion. I had limited contact with other new moms mainly because most of my friends had three or four children by the time I was having my first child. I discovered that sharing the joys and struggles of mothering doesn't always just happen naturally. During this difficult adjustment period, I often thought to myself, "I can't be the only one who feels challenged in this new role."

I believed God did not intend for mothers to live defeated, confused, or hopeless. I knew He desired mothers to be able to fulfill their roles with excellence, joy, and contentment. As I talked with other moms about my struggles, I soon realized that I was not unique in how I was feeling! Most of my friends had similar experiences with loneliness, uncertainty about their role, and physical exhaustion. I was greatly encouraged as I listened to my friends share biblical counsel, practical management strategies, and examples from their own mothering experiences. I learned that . . .

THE WISE WOMAN MANAGES MOTHERHOOD WITH EXCELLENCE

Her children rise up and bless her;
Her husband also, and he praises her.

PROVERBS 31:28

As a new mom, I remember having many doubts about my mothering abilities. I have developed the following principles as a result of my own struggle to adjust to my new role. Each day, they help me embrace with enthusiasm and purpose the blessing of being a mother. They also help guide my emotions, thoughts, and actions. I hope they will be an encouragement to moms of all ages. It is also my prayer that older women will be reminded that young mothers need their wisdom and encouragement. Share your stories, your joys, your fears, your challenges; let moms know they are not the only ones who have ever lacked confidence about their God-given role.

THE CULTURE SHOCK OF MOTHERHOOD

"For I know the plans that I have for you," declares the Lord,
"plans for welfare and not for calamity
to give you a future and a hope."
JEREMIAH 29:11

One of the first lessons I learned when I transitioned from working outside the home to working at home was that *motherhood changes every aspect of your life.* Change is difficult for most of us. Acknowledging that there are adjustments to be made when becoming a mother does not mean that you are less committed or less capable of performing your role. Motherhood really changed everything—what I ate, how I dressed, when I slept, what I read, the friends I had, the amount of time with my husband, and even how I handled my time with the Lord each day! In an attempt to try to keep my sense of humor during this adjustment period, I began to write down ways my life had changed. I began each sentence with, "You know you're a mommy when . . ." It helped me to see that most of the things that had changed were insignificant and not eternal in value—but they were still indicative of adjustments that needed to be made and pointed to why life often seemed unfamiliar and unorganized. Here is a sampling from my list; perhaps you can relate to a few of the changes I experienced!

You Know You're a Mommy When:

- "Sleeping late" on a Saturday morning is 7 A.M.!
- You get up on Sunday mornings at 5:30 A.M. and are still late for church!
- You know the location of every drive-through bank, pharmacy, and restaurant (so you don't have to do the car-seat-to-stroller/stroller-to-car-seat workout routine on every errand)!

- The grocery store is an exciting family outing!
- Weekly menu plans and recipes come from the *20 Minutes or Less* cookbook!
- You have your "quiet times" with the Lord during the 2 A.M. baby feeding!
- Macaroni and cheese or peanut butter and jelly sandwiches become your lunch delicacies!
- You discover you really can talk on the phone, give the baby his bottle, and play cars with your toddler all at once!
- You used to need an hour to get ready to go out but now are excited about having ten uninterrupted minutes to fix your hair and change your clothes!
- Staying up late is 9 P.M.!

Adjusting to motherhood is like adjusting to a new culture. It takes time, effort, and plenty of patience to feel comfortable in your new surroundings.

I also learned as a part of my adjustment to motherhood that any sacrifice, life change, or inconvenience, *pales in comparison* to the rich blessing and reward of becoming a mother. The depth of love I experience toward my children is like no other I have ever experienced. The rewards of watching them grow are priceless! I would not trade being at home with my boys as their mom for anything this world has to offer me. I often tell my boys, "You are mommy's gold!"

Becoming a mother is a *privilege*—not a *right* for a Christian woman. Because it is a privilege, the role of motherhood should be pursued *with excellence*. The desire to pursue motherhood with excellence led me to search the Scriptures in order to practically define what God expected from me as a mother. I did not want to just "survive" motherhood—I wanted to thrive and enjoy it. In order to enjoy it, I had to learn how to practically apply biblical truths to my daily "mommy" challenges.

⌒

GOD'S VIEW OF MOTHERHOOD

Behold, children are a gift of the Lord,
The fruit of the womb is a reward.
PSALM 127:3

The first place to begin when adjusting to our new role as mothers is to understand God's view of motherhood. We need to understand the significant responsibility God has entrusted us with when He gives us children. Since children are God's gifts to us, we should strive to be good stewards (found trustworthy) of His gifts (Psalm 127:3). Under the headship of their husbands, mothers have been placed by God in a unique position of influence in the lives of their children (Ephesians 5:22–6:4; Colossians 3:18–21). True, fathers will also have influence in their children's lives, but practically speaking, mothers who stay at home are able to spend more physical time with their children. Mothers learn the strengths and weaknesses of their children in intimate ways. This knowledge provides mothers the platform needed to train their children with wisdom.

What is child training? Reb Bradley defines child training as developing *maturity* in our children. Maturity can be seen in three areas:

- *Self-control:* not being ruled by passions, emotions, desires, wishes, or curiosity; freedom from having to do what one feels like doing; the ability to choose to do what is right; fostering the selflessness necessary to love others.
- *Wisdom:* understanding; insight; ability to learn from experience; ability to make sound decisions; handling stressful problems levelheadedly.
- *Responsibility:* accepting personal accountability for one's own actions; faithful and conscientious work habits; integrity and reliability.[1]

Why is training our children so important? Proverbs 22:6 says, "Train up a child in the way he should go, even when he is old he will not depart from it." Training our children to be self-controlled, wise, and submissive to parental authority helps them understand that we must also submit to God's authority. Hebrews 9:27 states, "It is appointed for men to die once and after this comes judgment." Our parenting (mothering) ought to reflect that our primary concern is the condition of our child's eternal soul, not just his or her physical needs. The greatest desire of a Christian mother's heart is to see her children come to know and love God. However, we know that only God can save our children (Ephesians 2:8–9). While there is nothing we can do to save our children or change God's plan for them, we *can* strive to be found faithful in loving, training, teaching, and witnessing to our children about Christ's sacrifice on the cross (John 3:16–18; 1 Corinthians 15:3–4).

The influence we have as mothers is why it is a *privilege* to be a mother—God Himself entrusted into our hands the incredible job of training, teaching, correcting, loving, and nurturing our children. Our passion for *mothering with excellence* should be born out of an understanding that we are stewards of our children before the Lord. It is a challenging question to ask, "What kind of influence am I on my children?"

THE IMPACT OF A MOTHER AT HOME

The rod and reproof give wisdom,
But the child who gets his own way
brings shame to his mother.
PROVERBS 29:15

Once we understand God's view of mothering we need to further discuss the value of being a mother who stays at home with her children. This is a controversial topic in our world today. It is not my intent to alienate women who are working outside the home—I, too, work part-time. My goal is to remind us of the *priority* that Scripture places on women managing their homes and caring for the needs of their families with *excellence.*

In order to fully appreciate the value of having a mother at home, we need to review God's design for the family. Husbands are to lead, love, and support their families, just as Christ loves His church (Ephesians 5:25–29; Colossians 3:19). Wives are to love their husbands and submit to their authority as they submit to Christ (Ephesians 5:22–24; Colossians 3:18). Children have one obligation in the family—to obey their parents (Ephesians 6:1–3; Colossians 3:20). God has clearly defined roles within the home for each member of the household. In addition to establishing *roles,* Scripture identifies specific *responsibilities* for husbands and wives to fulfill. For example, husbands are called to provide for the needs of their family (1 Timothy 5:8), love their wives as their own bodies (Ephesians 5:28), and bring up their children in the discipline and instruction of the Lord (Ephesians 6:4). Likewise, the woman's responsibilities are clearly defined in the Bible. Proverbs 31:10–31, Titus 2:3–5, and 1 Timothy 5:14 make it clear that women are to manage their homes with excellence, love their husbands, train their children, practice hospitality, and be involved in ministering to needy people. Reviewing Scriptures dealing with the woman's responsibilities makes it difficult to separate *mothering* from *homemaking.* Scripture defines the home as the main arena where the woman's influence will be most significantly felt.

When a woman chooses to work full-time outside the home she must be careful that she is not compromising what the Bible identifies as her *main priority*—her home and family. While Scripture does *not* forbid women to work outside the home, it does clearly identify many things women should be and do. A woman who chooses to work outside the home must be careful to select employment that will not cause her to compromise the priority of her family. It is noteworthy to mention at this point in our discussion that just because a woman is at home "full-time" *does not* mean she has kept her home and family as her priority. Women can still compromise the priority of their homes and family by overcommitting themselves to a variety of activities including volunteer work, hobbies, women's clubs, or even ministry obligations (for example, teaching Bible studies). While none of these activities is "wrong" for women to participate in, they still can cause women to compromise the priority of their home and family (just as outside employment can) because it divides her time and energy. *All* women need to carefully evaluate how much time and energy they give to any activity (whether paid employment or not). As mothers, we need to protect the priority of our home and family in all areas—time, energy, or thoughts. The woman who chooses to stay at home has the *potential* of giving her *best* time and energy to meeting the needs of her home and family. This is the value of a mother who stays at home.

HOMEMAKING WITH EXCELLENCE

The wise woman builds her house,
But the foolish woman tears it down with her own hands.
PROVERBS 14:1

Excellence can be defined as "unusually good quality."[2] There are several factors that enable women to manage their homes with excellence:

1. THE EXCELLENT HOME MANAGER IS TEACHABLE

It takes both *knowledge* and *skill* to manage a home with excellence. There are many areas women will need additional training to manage with excellence. Training may be formal (e.g., taking a class on food preparation) or informal (e.g., learning from an older woman or a book). Any and all education women receive can benefit the home and family. It does not matter what kind of home you were raised in—we all can *learn* to manage with excellence. Proverbs 1:7 says that "The fear of the LORD is the beginning of knowledge; fools despise wisdom and instruction."

2. THE EXCELLENT HOME MANAGER IS ORGANIZED

Your home will only be as organized as you are! Organization helps you "put in order" or "arrange" the various components of your life. Proverbs 31:27 reminds us that we are to "look well to the ways of [our] household." We do this with the help of the "tool" of organization. Your family will only be as organized as you are! There are several areas you need to organize in order to manage with excellence; they include organizing:

a. yourself (e.g., using a day timer or to-do list);
b. family calendar(s) (keep track of each person's commitments);
c. cleaning (e.g., establish a household cleaning schedule);
d. meals (e.g., routines for menu planning and grocery shopping); and
e. papers, mail, and "forms" (e.g., developing reusable "forms" for babysitters, shopping lists, or other areas used consistently saves time).

3. THE EXCELLENT HOME MANAGER IS FLEXIBLE

Flexibility means we are able to "adjust" or "bend without breaking." Becoming a mother has taught me much about flexibility. Children don't always follow "the plan" for the day. It is important to remember your children are your priority. We will have "many plans" (Proverbs 19:21) but the Lord will direct our days, and "interruptions" are usually not without purpose! We need to be flexible as we respond to the Lord's sovereign plan for each day.

4. THE EXCELLENT HOME MANAGER IS DEVOTED

Devotion implies that we are loyal and faithful. The primary means for demonstrating our devotion is by practicing Philippians 2:3: "Do nothing from selfishness or empty conceit, but with humility of mind regard one another as more important than yourselves." Becoming an excellent mom and home manager requires that we often place the needs of our family above our own desires. This is hard work! As a mother you will no longer have the comfort of being a "morning" or "night" person because you will be busy both morning and night (and in between)! Being a successful home manager requires a servant's heart and much personal sacrifice. A devoted mom is a faithful mom.

5. THE EXCELLENT HOME MANAGER IS MATURE

A successful home manager is one who is growing in her spiritual character. I have found no other experience has revealed sin in my life more than parenting. It has revealed selfishness, impatience, anger, and many other sinful traits in my heart. It can be very discouraging at times. However, the successful home manager learns from her mothering experiences and allows her role as a mother to stimulate her spiritual growth. Confessing my sin daily, seeking forgiveness from my family (including my children), and continuing to pursue Christlike character have become even more important in my role as a mother because I am a model for my children. I have learned that rather than allowing my failures as a mother to paralyze me with guilt, I need to allow them to stimulate me to change my character and grow in godliness. First Timothy 6:6 reminds us that "godliness actually is a means of great gain, when accompanied by contentment." Motherhood becomes the "tool" the Holy Spirit uses in my life to refine His fruit, as Galatians 5:22–23 describes: "But the fruit of the Spirit is love, joy, peace, patience, kindness, goodness, faithfulness, gentleness, self-control; against such there is no law."

6. THE EXCELLENT HOME MANAGER IS INTENTIONAL

Managing with excellence requires a *thoughtful* approach to mothering. Scripture says we are to "train up a child in the way he should go" (Proverbs 22:6). This implies that we give direction to the child's thoughts, attitudes, and actions. There are two broad categories for us to begin giving "intentional" thought to:

    a. Training our children—in practical and spiritual issues (remember we defined "training" earlier as bringing about maturity). Examples of the two areas would be:
        i) Practical issues—daily habits and/or attitudes such as good manners, respectful speech, or obedient responses;
        ii) Spiritual issues—knowledge of Scripture as well as modeling application through our own character.
    b. Educating our children—both academics and character issues. Whatever the method of education you choose for your child—public, private, Christian private, or homeschool—as parents we are called to be responsible for and involved in our child's education.

Something that has helped me be "intentional" on a daily basis is to remember three "Ps"—*pray, play,* and *practice.* Let me explain:

- **Pray**—I pray daily *for* my children as well as *with* my children. For example, I pray *for* my children that they will have a sincere and genuine faith in God and come to a saving knowledge of Him so He will be able to use them to further His kingdom. I pray that my children's character will be strong and mature. I like to pray through specific Scriptures and apply them to my children. For example, I have prayed through Philippians 2:14 for each of my children; "Dear Lord, please help (name of child) to learn to do all things without grumbling or disputing." Praying a specific Scripture for your children also helps you pray for their specific sin issues.

  I also try to pray *with* my children. Praying with my children allows me to model prayer. Our prayer times are not limited to before meals or naps; it is interwoven throughout our day as we *thank* God for our blessings (things like Daddy, Grandma, or favorite toys), pray for people we see who are injured in accidents as we are out driving, or pray after discipline has been administered as a part of restoring our relationship. Praying daily *for* and *with* your child not only models for them the importance of prayer, it also builds your relationship.

- **Play**—Play, of course, is a big part of any child's day! The most obvious form of play is "independent" playtime (where they can choose to play with whatever they like— some people call this "room time"). But in addition to regular playtime, I try to make sure I have played individually with each of my children. We usually pick one of their favorite activities like building blocks, racing cars, or throwing balls (I obviously have boys!). I have learned if I don't *make* the time to play, I never will because I am very task oriented, and there are always things "to do." Finally, playtime is also a learning time in our house. Sometimes we have "mommy-directed" playtime. I have them sit and read books, for example, or some other activity I have selected. I have found this to be important to teach self-control, have quiet play times, or to help keep my children occupied while I am completing a task (like talking on the telephone).

- *Practice*—Each week there are new "issues" my husband and I become aware of related to the training of our children. "Issues" vary depending on our child's age and temperament. Examples include: first-time obedience, feeding themselves, potty training, or demonstrating "happy hearts" (the term our family uses for having a good attitude). Whatever the "issue" is in our child's life, I try to be aware of it throughout the day and look for opportunities to "practice." Helping my child "practice" also keeps me more attentive to my child's individual needs (character and physical) and helps me be more intentional each day.

As a result of my desire to be "intentional," I developed a "parenting goals sheet" that helps remind me of the specific areas we are working on in our children's lives (see sample at the end of the chapter). My husband and I complete it together and keep it posted in a visible spot in our home. We include a "key verse" that applies to the areas we are working on (e.g., verses on patience, obedience, etc.) and a simple catechism question (e.g., who made the world?).

A catechism is simply an instruction guide. It is a handbook of questions and answers designed to teach principles of religion. To "catechize" children is to teach them to memorize the answers found in a catechism, so that when the catechism questions are asked, the children can reply with the correct responses. Because a good catechism is at the same time concise and thorough, when children have learned it well, their understanding of the basic doctrines of faith can be tested and found to be complete. One excellent catechism is the Westminister Shorter Catechism. In concise fashion, it gives children key biblical teachings about God, Scripture, the Lord Jesus Christ, the Holy Spirit, salvation, the sacraments, the Ten Commandments, and the Lord's Prayer.[3]

7. THE EXCELLENT HOME MANAGER IS GRACIOUS

She understands that she will retain her honor if she responds to people and life circumstances in a gracious manner (Proverbs 11:16). "Gracious" simply means the woman is "pleasant, kind, and courteous."[4] She is careful to communicate with respect to her husband and children. The result of graciousness is honor—meaning she is held in high regard. The reward for her labor and efforts to manage with excellence is honor.

I would encourage you to use the characteristics we have discussed as an evaluation tool:

- Am I teachable? (Proverbs 1:7)
- Am I organized? (Proverbs 31:27)
- Am I flexible? (Proverbs 19:21)
- Am I devoted? (Philippians 2:3)
- Am I mature? (1 Timothy 6:6)
- Am I intentional? (Proverbs 22:6)
- Am I gracious? (Proverbs 11:16)

Your response to these questions will give you insight into your strengths and weaknesses as a home manager. It will reveal areas needing further growth, just as there are areas in my life that need attention.

Now that we understand that excellence is our duty before the Lord, we need to discuss practical management strategies that will assist us in successfully managing the day-to-day aspects of home management and childcare.

PRACTICAL MANAGEMENT TIPS FOR MOTHERS

Encourage the young women to love their husbands,
to love their children, to be sensible,
pure, workers at home, kind,
being subject to their own husbands, so
that the word of God may not be dishonored.
TITUS 2:4–5

In the book of Titus, Paul instructs older women to "encourage" the younger women in their homemaking and child-rearing skills. What does it mean to "encourage?" *Encourage* can be defined as "giving courage, hope, or confidence; to urge on; to stimulate by helping or showing approval; giving support, promoting the development of."[5] This is an important principle for young wives and mothers to recognize—you have to *learn* the skills related to homemaking and mothering. I have learned much from older and more experienced women. A few years ago I began to make a list of practical management tips I learned either from other moms or through personal experience, and I hope they are encouragement to you! Every mom will need to adjust these ideas and develop distinct management strategies to meet the unique needs within her family.

1. REMEMBER THERE ARE SEASONS IN LIFE

Life will not always be demanding in the same way that it is when you have small children. The one thing I consistently hear mothers who have grown children say is, "Enjoy them, they grow up so fast." It's often very hard to *enjoy* our children when we have not slept through the night in three months, or we are lost in a pile of laundry stacked as tall as we are! It is really important, however, that we try to appreciate and enjoy the "small moments" of life—those precious moments that *only you as mommy* have the privilege of seeing. For example, you will probably be the one to see many of "the firsts" in your baby's life (first smile, first step, first word, etc.). You will be the one they run to for comfort and consolation. What a joy and privilege! Remember you are in a "season of life." This season will not last forever, so treasure it! You may find that starting a journal helps you to appreciate and enjoy this season in your life.

2. LEARN TO MAXIMIZE SMALL INCREMENTS OF TIME

It is highly unlikely that you will have large blocks of time to complete projects. Therefore, if you do not learn to use smaller segments of time, you will not complete big projects (e.g., housecleaning, paying bills, returning phone calls, etc.). Break large projects into smaller parts. Learning to maximize fifteen minutes at a time has helped me to accomplish much more on a daily basis.

3. ALLOW TIME FOR THINGS NOT ON YOUR TO-DO LIST

Every day I change diapers, empty the dishwasher, answer the phone, and numerous other things that take time but are not reflected on my list of things to do for the day. If I have not allowed "extra" time, it is easy to become impatient with my children and others who come my way. My joy is robbed, and I have forgotten my priority of lovingly training and meeting my children's needs (examples include: allowing time for potty accidents, traffic, or the extra time it takes to unload and load children in their car seats).

4. KNOW THE VALUE OF ROUTINE

Some women are naturally more structured than others, but all women will find that establishing routines will benefit their homes and children by time saved. For example, doing the laundry, housecleaning, or grocery shopping using a "routine" will save you time. Scheduling times for naps, eating, and other activities allows you to plan more accurately for errands, doctor's appointments, or getting together with friends. Children benefit from routines too, and often learn them very quickly. They help them know both what to expect in their day as well as what is expected of them (e.g., "nap times I put myself to sleep" or "room time I play with my toys," etc.). Having schedules has also helped me to know my children better. For example, I know to anticipate that my children will begin to be fussy usually about a half hour before their regular nap time. Even with routines built into life, a mother still needs to be able to be flexible on a day-to-day basis. No two days are exactly alike, but I have found that it is very rare when I cannot plan around my *general* routine—for example, planning around my children's nap times. Routines help keep my children a priority in my daily schedule, since I know that there are certain times of the day I need to be home for their benefit. I would encourage you to establish routines to bring order to your home.

5. BE A PREPARED MOTHER AND THINK AHEAD

Try to anticipate the items you need to take with you to make an outing away from home more pleasant for you and your children. In addition to a well-stocked diaper bag, I have learned to never leave the house without snacks, drinks, a book or toy, extra clothes (in case there are potty "accidents"), and jackets. There have been numerous times when having a snack or toy has helped pass the time during unexpected delays and comforted a tired or teething child!

6. DON'T NEGLECT THE WORD

It can be very difficult to "find a good time" to spend in God's Word. Having a personal time of prayer, meditation, and reading the Scriptures is imperative. If we neglect God's Word, how will we have wisdom to make decisions? How can we experience God's peace? And how can we be confident that we are thinking with discernment? You may find, as I did, especially in the early days of motherhood, that it is very difficult to have a quiet time. I remember working through this issue when my first son was born. Prior to his birth I would get up around 6 A.M. I would exercise, have a quiet time, get ready for work, eat breakfast, and be out the door by 8 A.M. However, when I first brought my son home from the hospital, I was finishing an early morning feeding right around 5 A.M., and the last thing I wanted to do was get up at 6 A.M. to exercise! You may have to adjust the "time" and "length" of your quiet time for a few weeks or months until your child settles down into routines for eating and sleeping. I would suggest that it is better to have fifteen minutes of consistent, daily time with the Lord than to wait until you have one full hour. We need to keep our minds renewed by meditating on God's Word (Romans 12:1–2). If we do not, we will quickly loose our joy, patience, and perseverance. There are many ways to maximize the brief moments of peace that are sprinkled throughout our day. I found using a devotional book during this time was a helpful tool because it kept me focused and was not overly time consuming. Whatever your method—protect your time with the Lord!

7. TAKE CARE OF YOURSELF PHYSICALLY

It is very easy as a new mom to neglect your personal health. For example, many times it is more important for me to take a nap while my children are napping rather than accomplish something on my to-do list (this was VERY hard for me to do at first!). But I have learned the value of being a rested mom rather than a frazzled mom! Other areas that should not be neglected are getting exercise and eating right. Taking appropriate time for these things will make you better prepared to meet the needs of your home and family. We all have physical limitations, and it is important to learn to work within the constraints the Lord has allowed in our lives. Many of us believe the lie of our American culture that tells us we can be all things and do all things. We cannot. We all have limitations on our time, energy, and resources. We must use biblical principles to discern our priorities for each of these areas.

8. MAINTAIN A "QUIET HOUR"

When your children are young, you will have "built-in" quiet hours during the day while they take their naps. However, even as your children get older, I would encourage you to maintain the principle of having a quiet hour sometime each day. They may not take naps, but they can play with toys in their rooms, read a book, or do some other quiet activity. This gives you time to take a nap yourself, make phone calls, write out a grocery list, or read God's Word. It also breaks the day up and gives you an opportunity to "refocus" for the rest of the day's activities.

9. GET HELP WHEN YOU NEED IT!

Some errands or appointments are really much easier to do without your children. It takes me longer to load the kids in and out of their car seats for some errands than it does to actually accomplish the task! It may be a better use of your time to wait until your husband can watch the children, and then run out for an hour to complete all your little errands at once. Swap babysitting with a friend or make personal appointments during times your husband is available to watch the children. It can also be refreshing to take a break from having your children with you. I know after even just an hour away from home I can't wait to see my children! The hugs and kisses that follow my return remind me just how much we love each other!

10. ADJUST YOUR HOME-MANAGEMENT STYLE

During every phase of life I have had to adjust how I accomplish the weekly tasks (things like cooking, cleaning, grocery shopping, and paying the bills). For example, I used to clean the house once a week in an uninterrupted two-hour block. I do not have an uninterrupted two-hour block of time now! I have to accomplish the housecleaning one task at a time, and it often takes more than one day to complete. Being flexible and adjusting "how" you accomplish tasks during each season of life is important to your success as a mother.

11. READ MORE ABOUT IT!

Reading not only provides practical advice for parenting, but it also keeps you motivated and encouraged to continue to "pursue with excellence" your role as a mother. Reading Christian books helps keep you focused on the biblical principles related to mothering. I know what you are thinking—*I don't have time to read!* I find it challenging to find time to read also, and this is another example of an area where I had to adjust my management strategy. I used to be able to read a whole chapter, or several chapters, in one sitting. Now I am thrilled when I can read a couple of pages at a time. I have learned, however, that it is still valuable to read just a few pages each day. I try to find one principle to apply from each time I have a chance

⌒

to read. Be consistent in reading a few pages each day, and before you know it, you will have read the whole book! Reading keeps your mind stimulated and your heart encouraged.

12. DETERMINE YOUR PRIORITIES

The world would have us believe that women can do all things. This is simply not true. We all have limited time and we all have differing amounts of energy. You must discern wisely how you will spend your time and energy. I don't spend a lot of time hanging out with girlfriends, reading fiction, having my nails done, going to tea, or many other things that I would enjoy. I simply do not have the time, and they do not reflect my most important priorities. I am also careful to evaluate things like ministry involvement. We need to be faithful to serve but not to the detriment of our families. When you are a new mom, you may have to minimize your ministry commitments for a season in order to meet the needs of your family. Eliminate the things you do not *have* to do.

13. MANAGE YOUR MEALS

One of the most challenging adjustments I made as a new mom was learning how to get dinner on the table with an infant in the house (an infant who seemed to always be fussy right around the time to start cooking dinner). Here are a few ideas I picked up along the way:

- *Use "quick cookbooks" to prepare menus.* Asking friends for their favorite "quick" recipes is also a good place to start.
- *Appliances can also help save work and time in your food preparation* (e.g., food processors, crockpots, pressure cookers, or bread machines).

- *When possible prepare "two recipes" and freeze the second for use at a later time.* There are many recipes that freeze well (spaghetti, lasagna, meatballs, cookies, and soups).
- *Start dinner in the morning.* Some simple preparation in the morning (perhaps during your child's morning nap) can help the dinner preparation go much faster. Also, there are many recipes that can be completely prepared in advance so you just have to put them in the oven. (I relied on many recipes like this when my children were infants because of feedings or fussy periods.)
- *Allow "extra time" for your food preparation.* I don't think this is unique to my household—but my children consistently had a "fussy time" starting around 5 P.M. We affectionately called it "having a meltdown"! I have learned to allow extra time so I can patiently manage the interruptions and give my children the needed "extra" attention. Sometimes I have to deal with discipline issues, and other times it is just nice to have extra time to read a book with my children.
- *Allow your children to participate in the meal preparation.* Not only does this develop their cooking skills, but it also develops their character as they learn to participate in family chores. When they are very young you can teach them to set the table rather than help cook the food.

14. KEEP ORGANIZED AND PLAN AHEAD

As a new mom you no longer have the luxury of figuring out your days as you go along. You now have another person completely dependent on you. If your day is unorganized, so is your child's. Figure out management systems that work for you. For some, a calendar in the kitchen will work well, for others it's a palm pilot or a simple to-do list. It does not really matter *how* you organize yourself and your family. The important thing is that you have taken the time to stay organized.

15. ACCOMPLISH ONE TASK A DAY

The needs of a new baby can be all-consuming. It is easy to feel overwhelmed with everything you need to accomplish each day—the never ending laundry, keeping the house clean and in order, preparing meals, grocery shopping and other errands can often be challenging to organize. I have found it very helpful to acknowledge that I cannot accomplish *everything* on my to-do list in one day without compromising my health and the needs of my family. I can, however, be faithful to accomplish *one* task a day—the laundry, grocery shopping, or part of the housecleaning.

16. CLEAN AS YOU GO

For some reason my home has a "pile" problem! Piles appear daily! Piles of laundry, toys, mail, books, and files to name a few! I have found that if I don't take the time to tidy up on a regular basis, the piles overtake our home! Here are two strategies I have found helpful:

- *Handle things once*—don't shuffle things around your house all day; put things where they belong the first time (this means everything has to have a place to go!). For example, when you collect the mail, sort it as you are looking through it. Put the trash in the trash can, put the bills in the bill file, and put personal letters by your stationery. I've even designated a place to put the mail that my husband needs to see. If you have a two-story house, there are probably piles of things downstairs that need to go upstairs! Place a basket on your stairs to collect them all and carry it up at the end of each day. Whatever your needs are, devise a system that helps you handle things once.

- *Pick up twice a day.* I find I cannot go all day without having to tidy up the house. I try to check the house twice a day. The first time is right after my children go down for their naps. I usually clean the kitchen, sweep or mop floors, put away books or other toys laying around the house, and clean up any other projects we have been working on that morning. It gives me a fresh start to the afternoon. In addition to this, I tidy up one more time right before my husband comes home. Your day may have been "frazzled," but you can still attempt to have a prepared and peaceful home for your husband to come home to. One way to communicate a peaceful home is to have an orderly home. Putting away toys and other unsightly piles of paper will make his welcome home even more comfortable!

17. LEARN FROM OTHERS

I have found it is always helpful to ask for advice from family and friends. I have asked for suggestions about various things, including how to feed my new baby, potty training, and discipline issues. Every time I seek the counsel of an older or more experienced mom I have reaped great rewards! I would encourage any new mom to find a few women she can call upon for counsel and advice related to mothering. (This might even include family members, like a sister or mother). I am like a dry sponge when I am around more experienced mothers; I want to learn from their successes and failures and soak up their wisdom that comes from their experience.

18. STAY ENGAGED WITH YOUR HUSBAND.

It is very easy, especially with a newborn, to become focused solely on your infant. They are very demanding and very dependent. However, meeting the needs of your child should not compromise your ability to meet the needs of your husband. It is critical to the health of your marriage relationship that you protect time for you to spend together—time for communication, praying, and just enjoying one another's company. You are still his "helpmate" even though you are a new mom. One simple thing I do to help keep him as my priority is ask him each morning before he goes to work if there is anything I can do for him that day. It is a simple habit, but it is one that I have found that helps me remember my "schedule" is not just about the kids and me!

A FINAL THOUGHT . . .

A few years ago my husband and I had the opportunity to visit England. I decided while we were traveling that I would read the biography of Susanna Wesley, mother of Charles and John.[6] It was fascinating to read the stories of her life and then see the actual locations of where the events took place. Even more captivating to me, however, was the powerful influence Susanna Wesley had on her children. She was the mother of nineteen children. She embodied the principles of mothering and managing with excellence! She took her role as a mother seriously. She prayed, trained, and educated each of her children. Susanna's life was very difficult—many of her children died (only nine lived to adulthood), and she lived in poverty and was often mistreated by the parishioners in their church (for example, their house was once burned down). Through it all, she remained a loyal and dedicated mother who modeled for her children a faithful and devoted commitment to God. What was her secret? I read that one was "throwing her apron over her head." Susanna obviously had a busy and noisy household (with at least nine children running around the home)! So she developed the habit of "throwing her apron over her head" during her prayer and devotion time with the Lord. Her children knew not to interrupt her under *any* circumstance. Susanna recognized the only way to be successful in her responsibilities as a wife and mother was to be completely dependent on God and His Word.

A woman's heart was made to support, love, and nurture her family. I would encourage you to value your role as a mother so you are willing to sacrifice for your family. I pray that we will be quick to "throw our aprons over our head" in order that we might be found faithful in our role as mothers.

GROWING IN
MANAGING MOTHERHOOD
WITH EXCELLENCE

1.   *Use the principles discussed in the "Homemaking with Excellence" section as an evaluation tool, and identify specific strategies for improving your home management. Ask yourself:*

- *Am I teachable? (Proverbs 1:7)*
- *Am I organized? (Proverbs 31:27)*
- *Am I flexible? (Proverbs 19:21)*
- *Am I devoted? (Philippians 2:3)*
- *Am I mature? (I Timothy 6:6)*
- *Am I intentional? (Proverbs 22:6)*
- *Am I gracious? (Proverbs 11:16)*

2.   *Read about the life of Susanna Wesley (either use the book listed in the endnotes section or select another of the many available). Observe specifically her:*

- *prayer habits,*
- *devotion to God,*
- *household management strategies, and*
- *methods for educating and training her children.*

Apply what you glean to your own life, home, and mothering.

3. Don't neglect the Word. Establish a time and place to spend with the Lord praying, reading His Word, and thanking Him for his many blessings in your life. There are many devotional guides and prayer books that will help you use your time effectively. Start by being consistent, then increase the length of time.

4. Remember the three "P's"—Play, Pray, and Practice. Identify which area you need to work on and develop strategies for making the needed changes. Here is one idea for each to get you started:

- *Play—Make an "activity list" of things you and your child enjoy doing together. You might find it helpful to make a list for "at home" activities and "away from home" activities. Keep this list handy and select activities each day or week to do individually with your children. Your list might look something like this:*

Name of Child	
Play activities at home	**Play activities away from home**
Build with blocks	Go to the park
Play with play dough	Ride the carousel
Read books together	Visit the farm animals
Play a board game	Ride the train

- *Pray—Select specific Scripture verses for each of your children. Personalize the verses by inserting your child's name. You might find it helpful to identify the specific sin issues in your child's life and then find appropriate Scripture dealing with their issues (e.g., fear, anger, unkind words, selfishness, etc.).*

- *Practice—Identify specific "growth goals" for your children's character and physical development.*

5. *Strive to become a more "intentional mom." One suggestion is to make a Parenting Goals Sheet for your children. Either use the following worksheet or develop your own "tool" that will help remind you of your parenting goals for your children. Goals may vary from person to person, but the principle is to develop a resource that helps you be intentional with your mothering!*

Start Date: _____

PARENTING GOALS FOR (*NAME OF CHILD*)

Wisdom Verse:

_____

_____

_____

Developmental Goals:

1._____

2._____

3._____

Character Goals:

1._____

2._____

3._____

Observations/Progress:

_____

_____

_____

Catechism Question for Review:

_____

_____

_____

End Date: _____

I attended college in sunny, southern California. Immediately following my college graduation, I was accepted into a graduate school in southern Nevada. I worked all summer saving for the expenses that I would incur during the fall semester. Right before moving to Nevada, I made an investment in a "real" winter coat. I did not really need a heavy winter coat in California, but I was about to spend two years near the Nevada Sierra Mountains, and it was going to be cold! Buying a new coat was a major expense for me at the time, and I remember carefully saving all summer so I would have enough money. I wore the full-length wool coat all winter long as I walked around campus in the snow. It was a blessing to have!

As the end of my first winter came and I was preparing to head home for the summer months, I had my coat dry-cleaned before storing it. A couple of days later, I picked up my coat and took it home to pack it away. As I removed the plastic covering I was shocked to see my coat looking like a scared cat! Little white threads were standing straight out all over my beautiful, black wool coat! The hem of the coat was now three inches shorter than the inner lining. My coat that once had been comfortably roomy in size was now difficult to button in the front. I was so disappointed and did not have the resources to replace it.

After giving my dilemma some thought, I remembered some of the textile and consumer education training I had received as a Home Economics major. My textile training said, "Check the fiber content label." It was labeled 100 percent wool. However, I knew the little white threads that were making my coat look like a scared cat were what we call "filling fibers" or, in other words, it was not 100 percent wool. The elastic "filling fibers" are found in lesser quality fabrics, not 100 percent wool. This was a mislabeled garment. My consumer training said, "Check the garment care label." It read, "Dry-clean Only." I had fulfilled my obligations as a consumer by following the care instructions. What was I to do? My consumer courses had also taught me that I needed to keep good records, including keeping receipts, so I had dutifully filed the receipt for the coat almost a year earlier. It was filed under "Major Purchases" in my simple filing system of a divided pocket envelope!

Later that week I took my receipt with the coat to the store where I had purchased it almost a year earlier. I reviewed my story with the sales clerk who referred me to the store manager. About a half hour later, I walked out of the store with a brand new coat! I was shocked—all the textile and consumer training I had received actually worked! Today, I still file all receipts and keep them for at least a year! I learned several valuable lessons through my "winter coat" experience. First, and most important, the Lord does provide for all our needs. Second, He sometimes uses our faithfulness of being a good steward to provide for those needs. I learned that . . .

THE WISE WOMAN IMPLEMENTS STEWARDSHIP

Therefore if you have not been faithful
in the use of unrighteous wealth,
who will entrust the true riches to you?

LUKE 16:11

Having a basic knowledge of how to be a good consumer is critical to managing your money with excellence. As we strive to be found faithful stewards of the resources God has placed in our lives, there will be many decisions to make and alternatives to choose from regarding how we use our resources. To be a *steward* means we are the supervisor or administrator of God's resources. Acknowledging we are stewards for God helps us to remember that "every financial decision is a spiritual decision."[1] Our primary motivation for practicing good stewardship is so we will be found *faithful* with whatever God has given to us—time, energy, money, or abilities (1 Corinthians 4:2).

Good means our management has been superior, excellent, or of high quality; while *faithful* implies we have been a loyal and trustworthy manager.

Becoming good stewards of God's resources requires that we develop financial management skills and consumer spending skills so that we are making wise decisions. In chapter six of *Becoming a Woman Who Pleases God,* we laid the foundation for biblical financial management. It is important that these areas are reviewed. You need to know what God's Word says about money (biblical financial principles), how to manage your resources (developing financial management skills), how to organize and monitor your spending (basic budgeting skills), and finally, if you are married, be like-minded with your husband about how to manage your finances (partnering with your spouse on finances). Let's build on these concepts by identifying some practical steps to developing good consumer decision-making skills.

PRACTICING RESPONSIBLE CONSUMERISM

Wealth obtained by fraud dwindles,
But the one who gathers by labor increases it.
PROVERBS 13:11

Being a good consumer requires that you have both the knowledge and skills to make prudent financial decisions. While there is much that could be addressed under this topic, we are going to focus on eight areas. Improving our knowledge and execution of these principles helps us become better consumers, and ultimately, better stewards of God's resources.

1. KNOW HOW TO SHOP

Even though women are often known as "shoppers," we don't all know *how* to shop! A few guidelines include:

- *Remember your budget.* You need to decide before you leave your house how much you can spend. Know what you can and cannot afford. You might need to delay a purchase in order to save before purchasing a particular item.
- *Conduct appropriate research.* Know what features you *need* and *desire.* Needs are nonnegotiable features, and desires are things that would be nice if you can afford them. Nowadays, most of this research can be done over the Internet to save you time.
- *Always practice comparison-shopping.* I would encourage you to compare at least three different sources before making a purchase. Compare the features from the information you collected while conducting your research. You might find it helpful to prepare a *comparison-shopping worksheet.* List the features you are shopping for in a column on the left side of your paper and then list the three sources across the top. For example, if I needed to purchase auto insurance, my comparison-shopping worksheet might look something like Table 6.1:

TABLE 6.1 COMPARISON-SHOPPING WORKSHEET			
Kind of Coverage/ Limits	Company #1	Company #2	Company #3
Bodily Injury			
Property Damage			
Comprehensive			
Collision			
Medical Payments			
Uninsured Motorist			
Personal Injury			
Emergency Road			
Total Premium			

The time it takes to prepare a worksheet is well worth the potential savings. Also, the information helps you understand exactly what you are purchasing. Comparison-shopping can include: comparing brand names, asking for word-of-mouth recommendations, and looking at formal product evaluations, like consumer reports from non-profit product testing agencies. Developing the habit of comparison-shopping will help prevent impulse buying, a common consumer mistake. Whether the item you are shopping for is a simple summer dress or a new computer system, you will always benefit from comparison-shopping.

- *Read and compare warranties.* It is important to check warranties so you know what the manufacturer will take responsibility for and what you are responsible for. The warranty will explain how you are to handle repairs and will state how long the warranty is in effect.
- *Understand all contracts before signing.* Make sure you take the time to actually read a contract before signing it. If there is something you do not understand, ask the salesperson to explain it before you sign it. Also, never sign a contract with blank spaces; check to see that all the information has been completely filled in. Ask for a copy of the contract if they do not offer you one before leaving the store.
- *Be familiar with the store's return or exchange policy.* Some stores never give cash back for example; they only issue store credit. Other companies have a limited time during which they will accept returns.

2. KNOW WHERE TO SHOP

There are a variety of retail options available to consumers, including: department stores, specialty stores, discount stores, factory outlets, Internet companies, and secondhand shops. They each offer different advantages and disadvantages (e.g., return policies, merchandise selection, quality of goods, and prices). You should select the location of where you shop based on the merchandise you are purchasing. For example, you may prefer to purchase appliances from a specialty store so there are knowledgeable salespeople and good customer services (e.g., warranties, repair policies, etc.). On the other hand, visiting a factory outlet may be a good choice for purchasing certain clothing items that do not need warranties, etc.

3. KNOW WHEN TO SHOP

Become a "seasonal" shopper! Learning to plan ahead to take advantage of the seasonal sales or promotions can save you a lot of money. Seasonal clothing, sports equipment, appliances, or gifts are available in greater quantity and variety early in the season, but the prices will usually be lower at pre-, mid-, or end-of-season sales. You can also take advantage of "holiday" sales (e.g., Fourth of July or Christmas sales). Finally, take advantage of the traditional calendar sales for the specific item you are purchasing (for example, linens usually go on sale in January, china dishes in June, and autos in September). Seasonal shopping simply requires planning in advance.

4. KNOW WHAT TO DO AFTER YOU MAKE A PURCHASE

Once we make our purchases it is easy to forget we still have several steps to complete in order to ensure we are protected if there is a problem with a product. For example, an appliance may stop working before the warranty ends. Following a few simple steps will help keep you organized; they include:

- Develop a simple filing system for receipts, warranties, and user manuals (be sure to use it once you establish it!). Keep all documentation.
- Complete and return warranty information (you have to register the warranty information to initiate it and give the company a record of your purchase). Remember if you have a problem, you may have additional warranty rights in your state (you can check with your local or state consumer office).
- Read and follow the care instructions and user directions.
- Use the product only as the manufacturer recommends.
- Report any problems as soon as they occur (don't try to fix the problem yourself; this may actually cancel the warranty).
- Keep photocopies of all letters or correspondence when trying to resolve problems (don't send original receipts). Instructions for writing a complaint letter and how to resolve disputes are discussed later in the chapter.

5. KNOW HOW TO BE A CONSCIENTIOUS CONSUMER

It is a blessing to live in America for many reasons; one is the consumer protection laws established for its citizens. We often take these laws and regulations for granted, forgetting that it is only because we live in America that we can expect merchandise to be safe or that we have avenues for resolving problems with faulty products (this is not true for many countries around the world). These consumer "rights" as they are known were first established in the 1960s by President Kennedy (and have been added to by subsequent presidents) to help protect American consumers and ensure they achieve the most for their money.

Your consumer rights include: the right to safety, to be informed, to choose, to be heard, to a decent environment, to consumer education, and to reasonable redress for physical damages suffered when using a product. American consumers also have certain *responsibilities* they are expected to fulfill: giving correct information, reporting defective goods, reporting wrongs incurred in consumer dealings, obeying the law when protesting, and accepting the consequences of their consumer decisions.

Being a *conscientious consumer* means that I am practicing with integrity and truthfulness my rights and responsibilities in the marketplace. *Conscientious* can be defined as "careful to do what one knows is right; controlled by conscience."[2] I am sure you have heard the saying "with privilege comes responsibility." This is the principle we are emphasizing here. For example, it is a privilege to have "consumer rights," so I should be faithful to stay informed, conduct research, make my consumer opinions known, and seek recourse for faulty merchandise. Additionally, I need to be an honest consumer (e.g., reporting correct information and obeying the law). If I do not practice both my rights and responsibilities, I have not been a conscientious consumer. For example, if I fail to report faulty merchandise, then someone else will experience the same inconvenience of returning the product or might be injured by the product. Because of the high standard of conduct God calls us to in His Word, Christians should be the most conscientious consumers in the marketplace.

6. KNOW YOUR CONSUMER RESOURCES

The Internet provides immediate access to any kind of information we need to be effective consumers. I would encourage you to take advantage of the wealth of information that is available to you; it will help you stay informed and make better decisions with your financial resources. While there are numerous consumer resources available, one very helpful resource that consolidates most of the information you might need is the *Consumer Action Handbook*. One free copy per person is available each year from the Consumer Information Center (www. pueblo.gsa.gov or call 1-888-878-3256). In addition to the *Consumer Action Handbook* you can order a free copy of the *Consumer Information Catalog* which lists hundreds of free or low-cost federal publications on consumer interests, including: food, nutrition, health, mortgages, credit, automobiles, travel, education, finances, and many other topics. As well, there is a brief listing of important consumer Web sites at the end of this chapter (see Table 6.4).

7. KNOW HOW TO RESOLVE A PROBLEM

It is inevitable that we will experience problems with merchandise or services in our marketplace. As a part of good stewardship, we ought to be competent at following the correct procedures for resolving problems. Most importantly, we must remember that we should never compromise our testimony when seeking to resolve a dispute (we will discuss this more under point eight). We should always be courteous, honest, and patient while resolving consumer problems. If you have a complaint against a merchant or their merchandise follow these procedures:

- After purchasing a product save all documentation: sales receipts, operating manuals, copies of warranties, and the name of the salesperson (start a file for each purchase and keep all the paperwork together).
- If the product proves to be faulty or defective, call or visit the place of purchase. Talk to the salesperson about the proper procedures for obtaining a refund, getting the product repaired or replaced.
- If you are unsuccessful at obtaining the service you are requesting, ask to speak to the manager.

- If you are unsuccessful with the manager, you can do all of the following: write the president or chairperson of the company (visit your local library to find the name and address), write to local and state consumer groups about your problem, and contact national consumer-help agencies or consumer action-panels. All letters should include copies (not originals) of your paperwork (receipts, other letters you have written, etc.).
- If you still do not resolve your problem, you can contact your state attorney general's office. Writing a complaint letter should never be sarcastic, rude, or dishonest. It should provide the necessary information to help the company or manufacturer resolve your complaint. It should also provide your supporting documentation (see Table 6.5 for an example of a complaint letter).

8. KNOW HOW TO BE A CHRISTIAN FIRST AND A CONSUMER SECOND

It is very important that we remember in all of our consumer or financial dealings that we are managing God's resources—not our own. As Christians, this should be a good motivator to not compromise our testimony in any of our attitudes or actions. Our character should set us apart from unbelievers in the marketplace. There are three character traits that will help protect us from compromising our testimony:

- *Honesty*—Proverbs 16:8 states, "Better is a little with righteousness than great income with injustice." God expects us to act with truthful integrity in all of our business dealings and financial transactions (Proverbs 20:7). He expects us to labor for our wealth (Proverbs 13:11).
- *Gracious Speech*—This implies we are courteous, kind, and not sarcastic or rude with our words. God calls us to

demonstrate kindness, tenderheartedness, and forgiveness—even to those who have wronged us (Ephesians 4:32).
• *Self-control*—There may be many times when we are "le-
gitimately" wronged because of faulty merchandise or in-
competent service. Christians, however, are called to
demonstrate self-control that is a fruit of the Spirit (Galatians 5:22–23). This character trait, or fruit, is produced
as I grow in my relationship with God. Practicing self-control as a consumer means that I am restrained with my
emotions, I am demonstrating patience, and I avoid becoming angry.

A part of practicing good stewardship does require us to
know how to resolve complaints and correct errors in our financial dealings. However, we do this within the boundaries
of our Christian character. Sometimes this means we will not
always "get the best deal," have our complaints resolved, or
utilize every legal means available to us as American consumers.
It takes wisdom and discernment to know what is appropriate and what will compromise our testimony (Proverbs
8:12–14; 24:3–4).

DISTINGUISHING BETWEEN CONSUMERISM AND CHRISTIAN CHARACTER

No one can serve two masters;
for either he will hate the one and love the other,
or he will be devoted to one and despise the other.
You cannot serve God and wealth.
MATTHEW 6:24

Now that we have discussed several practical steps to guide
our financial decision making, we need to take some time to
think about what it means to be a consumer and then what it
means to be a Christian and a consumer. The term *consumer*

is a very American term and concept. Consumers can be defined as "individuals who purchase (or are given), use, maintain, and dispose of products and services in their final form in an attempt to achieve the highest level of satisfaction possible with their income limitation."[3] As we discussed earlier, because we live in America we have certain consumer *rights* and *responsibilities*. Unfortunately, however, it is very easy for us to transfer our American consumer mentality of rights into our Christian walk. There is a great danger in applying "consumer attitudes" to all areas of our lives. Consumer skills, rights, and responsibilities should be applied in ways that keep with *good financial stewardship*. As Christians, consumer "rights" cannot be applied to our relationships with people, our attitudes toward our church, or to the interactions with the authorities in our lives without violating principles that God has outlined clearly in His Word (such as submitting to authorities and loving others selflessly). By comparing the consumer focus of "rights" with the biblical focus of "character" you can see we need to be careful to acknowledge consumer skills are just *tools* to help us make good financial decisions within our economy, not attitudes for our life in general. There is no place for a "consumer mentality" in Christianity.

TABLE 6.2	
CONSUMER FOCUS COMPARED WITH A BIBLICAL FOCUS	
CONSUMER FOCUS **Rights and Skills**	BIBLICAL FOCUS **Character and Attitudes**
Rights—Consumers believe they deserve certain rights and seek to get what they deserve.	*Selflessness*—Christians consider others before themselves (Romans 12:10; Philippians 2:3).

TABLE 6.2 (cont'd) CONSUMER FOCUS COMPARED WITH A BIBLICAL FOCUS	
CONSUMER FOCUS **Rights and Skills**	BIBLICAL FOCUS **Character and Attitudes**
Protection—Consumers place their faith in government laws and regulations.	*Provision*—Christians place their faith in God's sovereignty and ability to provide for our needs (Psalm 56:4; 73:28).
Correction—Consumers believe they deserve justice and fairness.	*Sin and an Evil World*—Christians know there will never be total fairness in this world (Psalm 34:16; Proverbs 11:1–6; Jeremiah 17:9–10; Ephesians 5:15–17).
Responsibilities—Consumers focus on what they are required to do.	*Character*—Christians focus on who they are, not what they do (Romans 5:1–5; Galatians 5:22–23).
Scarcity—Consumers seek to maximize their resources to get "the most" for themselves.	*Stewardship*—Christians acknowledge they do not own anything, they are managers (Psalm 24:1–2; Romans 14:8; 1 Peter 4:10).
Service—Consumers demand satisfaction with products, goods, or services.	*Servanthood*—Christians lay down their "rights" (Proverbs 17:2; Matthew 20:25–28; John 12:23–26).

We see the "consumer mentality" reveals itself in many areas of our lives; here are some of the ugly examples:

• Promoting self rather than considering the needs of others.

- Being unsubmissive to the leadership God has placed in your life (for example, the authority of the church, employers, or husbands).
- Always demanding fairness or justice.
- Becoming consumed with worry and forgetting that God has promised to provide for my needs.
- Evaluating relationships, Christian ministries, church services, or even the pastor's preaching by the subjective standards of "how it made me feel" or "what I got out of it" rather than evaluating their correspondence with God's Word.

Becoming a good consumer is an admirable goal for practicing faithful stewardship. However, it is important to remember that consumer principles, when applied wrongly to your Christian walk, will compromise your Christian character and ultimately your Christian testimony to others. Remember, you are a Christian before you are an American consumer!

PLANNING FOR THE FUTURE

*There is precious treasure
and oil in the dwelling of the wise,
But a foolish man swallows it up.*
PROVERBS 21:20

The last important component of being good stewards with the resources the Lord gives us is planning for our futures. Scripture tells us clearly that we should not be spending or consuming all that we have (Proverbs 21:20). God uses the example of the ant to remind us that we should be "storing up" for the future (Proverbs 6:6–11; 30:24–25). We ought to acknowledge that God is in control of our future, but at the same time we should be thoughtfully planning for it (Proverbs 16:9). There are five general areas to consider: saving, insurance, investing, retirement planning, and estate planning. Let's briefly consider each of these areas.

1. SAVING

The first practical step in planning for the future is to not spend everything that you make. It is important that we regularly set aside money for "future use." This money will be used for a variety of needs throughout our lifetimes; for example, we may experience various emergencies, lose our jobs, desire to meet a specific need someone else has, or pay for our children's college education. Whatever the use, the principle is to save for future needs. I would encourage you to build into your budget a specific percentage that you set aside for saving (working toward a minimum of 10 percent is a good starting point). Then you can decide what you are saving for and where you would like to "store" your money (what kind of savings account or savings tools). You probably will not be able to save for every area you would like all at once, but as you accomplish one goal you can move on to the next. The principle is that you develop the habit of saving. Some ideas for savings goals might include:

- *Unexpected Expenses:* Saving a monthly amount for *unanticipated* expenses like car repairs or dental work. A good goal is to save approximately $1,000 – 2,500 for minor emergencies.
- *Emergency Expenses:* It is prudent to establish a *major* emergency account with a minimum of three to six months salary in case of a long-term illness or job loss.
- *Giving Fund:* A giving fund allows you to give above and beyond your monthly tithes and offerings. This fund can be used to meet unexpected needs of the people God has placed in your life (e.g., friends who have a death in the family or special needs of missionaries). You may want

to have this as a part of your monthly budget (for example, fifty dollars every month is given away or accumulated for meeting larger needs).

- *Vacation Fund:* Saving each month toward your family vacation will allow you to use cash and avoid credit. This amount will vary depending on how frugal you are on vacation!

- *Specific, Long-term Goals:* Saving toward a down payment on a home, paying for your children's college education, or retirement plans.

2. INSURANCE

Life, disability, and various forms of supplemental medical insurance (e.g., for cancer) are tools you can use to meet the needs of your family in the future. There may be some Christians who feel the use of insurance (particularly life) compromises the principle of trusting God to provide for our needs. I would suggest, however, that life insurance or supplemental disability insurances are simply additional financial tools we can use to provide for the needs of our families (especially in the event of our death). I would also suggest that our attitude as Christians toward the use of insurance should be different than the world's view. For example, the world's perspective tends to focus solely on *protection* from risk (risk from perils like major disasters, accidents, or death). Merely focusing on protection from our insurance may cause us to be "insurance poor" as we attempt to protect families and ourselves from every calamity in the world.

Our perspective as Christians should be to focus on *provision* for our family. We know we are not in control of the circumstances of our lives, but we know the One who is in control of our lives and He promises to provide for our needs (Matthew 6:34). We are commanded to plan for the future and work with

God to provide for the needs of our families (1 Timothy 5:8). Scripture promises us that diligent planning leads to plenty (Proverbs 21:5). After we have established our emergency saving funds, the next step in planning for the future might be to secure life insurance (or other disability or supplemental health insurance depending on your circumstances). Typically, the first question relating to life insurance is, "How much do I need?" The general rule of thumb is approximately 75 percent of income lost until age sixty-five (for the person being insured) or about two to six times the amount of your annual income (depending on how much you make (two for higher incomes and six for lower incomes). More specifically, you should determine what you would like to provide for your family and use these goals to determine how much life insurance you need to obtain. Here are a few questions to consider to help you determine your goals:

- How much do I need to replace lost income?
- What will be the final expenses (e.g., funeral, estate fees, outstanding debts, etc.)?
- How much will my family need for the readjustment period? (For example, if your spouse works you may want to provide for a period of time where he/she does not have to work.)
- What debts will need repayment?
- How many dependents do I have, and do I want my spouse to be able to stay at home with them until the youngest is eighteen years old?
- What other expenses are related to my dependents (e.g., special health considerations, college educations, weddings, etc.)?
- What taxes will I owe?
- What other assets do I own that will help meet the needs of my family in addition to insurance (e.g., savings or investments)?

Once you determine how much life insurance you need, you may not be able to purchase the entire amount all at once (for example, a young family may need life insurance but may not be able to purchase the amount they calculate by considering the above questions). If this is the case, begin purchasing small amounts and add to it or convert your policies as your finances allow. One final thought about life insurance—typically we focus on purchasing life insurance for the main breadwinner (usually the husband); however, I would encourage you to consider purchasing life insurance for the wife as well—especially if she is a stay-at-home mother. The services she provides for her family are very costly to replace (for example, child care, housecleaning, meal preparation, or running errands). In the event a wife and mom should die before her children are raised, it can help with the additional expenses.

3. INVESTING

Relying on regular savings accounts will generally not be the best use of our savings dollars. There are many financial tools that will allow us to earn an interest rate that will help us keep up with or surpass the inflation rate. The most important principle here is that we understand the *power of compounding interest*. Saving a little bit consistently adds up over time, and it is important that we begin to save and invest as soon as possible because we can save smaller amounts to accomplish the same goals if we start early (see Table 6.3).

Before you begin investing your money in long-term saving tools you should establish an emergency fund, secure appropriate amounts of life insurance, and be able to afford *not* to access the money you are investing for several years. When the time comes to invest I would encourage you to meet with a qualified, experienced, licensed, financial planner or counselor to develop a long-term investment plan. They will be able to help

TABLE 6.3	
POWER OF COMPOUNDING INTEREST	
Time	$10,000 at 10 Percent Interest Will Be Worth
10 years	$ 25, 936
20 years	$ 41, 770
30 years	$ 67, 272
40 years	$108, 342

you determine the best investment tools to help you accomplish your goals with the appropriate level of risk for you.

Before you begin investing your money in long-term saving tools, you should establish an emergency fund, secure appropriate amounts of life insurance, and be able to afford *not* to access the money you are investing for several years. When the time comes to invest I would encourage you to meet with a qualified, experienced, licensed, financial planner or counselor to develop a long-term investment plan. He or she will be able to help you determine the best investment tools to help you accomplish your goals with the appropriate level of risk for you.

4. RETIEMENT PLANNING

While we may desire to remain active until our death, it is inevitable that our age will limit the amount of energy and stamina we have to spend being employed. The main question that usually arises when thinking about retirement planning is "How much will I need?" The general rule of thumb is to plan on between 70 and 80 percent of your pre-retirement monthly income if you desire to maintain a comparable standard of living. You should consider your unique circumstances to make a more exact estimate; for example, your health condition, if you have a spouse working, and changes in your expenses after you retire. You should plan on meeting your retirement expenses from a *variety* of sources, including:

- Company retirement plans (approximately 18–20%)
- Social Security (approximately 20–22%)
- Salary/earnings (approximately 22–24%)
- Investments and savings (approximately 34–36%)
- Miscellaneous (approximately 2%)

You may not divide your retirement income into the same percentages as suggested above, but you should begin to think through the various sources of income for your retirement years.

5. ESTATE PLANNING

Estate planning is important for two reasons: first, because with proper planning we can legally protect the wealth we have accumulated from needless taxes and other costs related to changing ownership of property. Second, estate planning allows us to be good stewards even in our death. We can determine in advance how we desire our assets to be distributed. Some of you may be thinking that estate planning is only for the wealthy. Not so! Estate planning is for everyone and it is a part of good stewardship. Scripture is clear that we brought nothing into this world, and we will take nothing out (1 Timothy 6:7). We need to remember our days are numbered and plan appropriately (Psalm 90:12). We can provide for our families even in the event of our death by taking the time to plan ahead (1 Timothy 5:8). Here are a few things to consider with your estate planning:

- *Provide for your family* (1 Timothy 5:8).
- *Continue to give to God in your death* (e.g., your church, parachurch organizations, missions, etc.).

- *Be prepared.* Have an inventory of your possessions and a list of where your assets are located.
- *Draw up a will and/or living trust to pass on your estate* (living trusts will avoid many of the estate taxes and fees; consult a lawyer for more information regarding the laws in your state).
- *Identify a guardian for your dependents.*
- *Discuss your plans with your spouse and family.* Make them aware of your desires and what they should do in the event of your death (make sure they know where your assets are, who your lawyer is, etc.).
- *Plan for* probate *(fees for wills).* Protect your family from owing money or acquiring debt when you die.

A FINAL THOUGHT . . .

As consumers we all have very different life circumstances. We have different levels of education, consumer knowledge, income, family sizes, resources where we reside, and health conditions, to name a few. However, if we are Christians, we all should have a common goal—we should be striving to be found faithful or trustworthy as stewards (1 Corinthians 4:2). I am reminded of the parable of the talents found in Matthew 25:14–30 where each individual was given responsibility for differing amounts of money. The amounts of money were not of concern to the master. Their responsible stewardship and faithful management was what caused the master to say, "Well done, good and faithful slave. You were faithful with a few things, I will put you in charge of many things; enter into the joy of your master" (Matthew 25:21, 23). May we always remember that this is the goal of practicing informed and skilled consumerism—to be found faithful stewards who can enter into the joy of our Master.

GROWING IN
IMPLEMENTING STEWARDSHIP

1. *Review the standards for our character outlined in Scripture. Identify the character traits followed by how you can practically "live out" or apply this trait. Use the chart below to start and then add passages of your own.*

Scripture Passage	Character Traits Identified	Application Ideas
Galatians 5:22–23		
Philippians 2:1–11		
Colossians 1:9–12		
2 Peter 1:5–8		

2. *Evaluate if your have allowed the "consumer mentality" to creep into your Christian walk. Ask yourself the following questions, and then identify any changes you need to make to practice the Christian character traits identified in your table above.*

- *Am I humble and considerate of the needs of others?*
- *Am I submissive to authority (e.g., employer, government, or church)?*

- *Am I easily angered because I expect justice and fairness in every area of life, even though I know we live in an imperfect and sinful world?*
- *Am I critical of others based on my personal opinions or feelings, or do I evaluate others based on their character and God's Word?*

3. *Identify the next major purchase you are planning. Prepare a Comparison Shopping Worksheet to help you in your decision making. List the desired features in a column on the left side and the three sources for comparison across the top of the page.*

4. *Organize your filing system—put receipts, warranties, and user manuals in your files together.*

5. *Begin planning for your future. Select one of the areas discussed—saving, insurance, investing, retirement planning, or estate planning—and complete the following:*

- *Research the planning tools available to you as a consumer (e.g., various types of bank accounts, investment tools, or forms of insurance).*
- *Get professional advice—ask questions based on your research.*
- *Set goals and establish a plan for implementing your goals.*
- *Implement your goals and start making progress toward planning for your future!*

TABLE 6.4
CONSUMER RESOURCE LIST

Agency Name	Web Address	Topical Information
American Arbitration Association	www.adr.org	Third–party intervention, settles disputes before courts
Better Business Bureau (BBB)	www.bbb.org	Provides information on local businesses; arbitration services
Bureau of Labor and Statistics	www.stats.bls.gov	Employment trends; prepares consumer price index (CPI)
Center for Disease Control (CDC)	www.cdc.gov	Information on specific diseases or health issues
Consumer Information Center	www.pueblo.gsa.gov	Provides Consumer Resource/Action Handbook and free consumer information; provides free federal publications
Consumer Product Safety Commission	www.cpsc.gov	Product safety and hazards
Consumer's Union	www.consumer reports.org	Publisher of Consumer Reports; nonprofit organization; private product testing
Direct Marketing Association	www.dmaconsumers. org/consumer asistance.html	How to get your name off mailing, telemarketing, and e-mail lists
Federal Reserve Board	www.federal reserve.gov	Information about banking and credit

Agency Name	Web Address	Topical Information
Federal Trade Commission (FTC)	www.ftc.gov	Advertising; fraud; mail-order problems; warranties; enforces standards
Food & Drug Administration (FDA)	www.fda.gov	Issues related to food, drugs, and cosmetics
Internal Revenue Service (IRS)	www.irs.gov	Federal tax information; provides resources for tax questions
National Automotive Dealers Association (NADA)	www.nada.org	Car shopping tips, dealer finder, reviews, and lemon check
National Association of Attorneys General (NAAG)	www.naag.org	Links consumers to their state Attorney General office
National Foundation for Credit Counseling (NFCC)	www.nfcc.org	Provides free credit counseling and financial planning assistance
National Institute of Standards & Technology (NIST)	www.nist.gov	Tests the efficiency or safety of products
United States Department of Agriculture (USDA)	www.usda.gov	Inspects and grades meat and poultry; how to spend food dollars
United States Postal Service	www.usps.gov	Mail fraud; unordered merchandise, obscenity in mail

Note: Each agency listed above provides information on numerous additional topics; the list above is just a sampling to get you started.

TABLE 6.5
SAMPLE COMPLAINT LETTER

Your Name
Address
Telephone Number

Date

Addressee (Company President, Chairperson, or Manager)
Company Name and Department (if applicable)
Street Address
City, State, Zip Code

Dear Sir or Madam:

I am writing this letter to inform you of my dissatisfaction with *(name the product with serial number or the service performed)*, which I purchased *(the date and location of purchase)*.

My complaint concerns *(the reason(s) for your complaint)*. I have attempted to resolve this matter by *(identify the steps already taken)*. I am writing to request *(state the specific action you desire to resolve your problem—return, refund, or replacement)*.

Thank you in advance for considering my request. I look forward to hearing from you in a timely manner. I will allow three weeks for a reply before *(state the next appropriate step in resolving this matter; for example, writing consumer agencies)*.

Sincerely,

Your Name
(Sign your name above the typed name)

Enclosures: *(Include copies [not originals] of all supporting documentation)*

As a child, celebrations were important in the Ennis household. I clearly recall the January 31st that I arrived home and found the dining room table set with Mom's best linens and china. Lying across my bed was a new fancy dress, and my favorite black, patent leather shoes were awaiting my feet. I was ten. I was helped to get ready, and when Dad arrived, he stayed in his best suit. The special dinner was served.

My parents explained many things to me but did not feel obligated to give exensive details or try to make a child understand all of their adult decisions. They were very wise in this way. My parents had thoughtfully planned this occasion and began explaining an important decision they had made. January 31st was the day that they had brought me home from the hospital, six months after my birth. I was not their birth child, but I was very special, because they had chosen me. That evening we were celebrating the day that I joined the Ennis family. Their explanation made my later transition to salvation smooth, since salvation was described to me as being adopted into God's family. How could I not desire salvation when the first adoption was so wonderful?

Though this celebration was a very important one, it was not an isolated event; hospitality was practiced regularly in our home because my dear mother knew that . . .

SEVEN

THE WISE WOMAN CULTIVATES A HOSTESS' HEART

Let love be without hypocrisy.
Abhor what is evil; cling to what is good.
Be devoted to one another in brotherly love;
give preference to one another in honor;
not lagging behind in diligence,
fervent in spirit, serving the Lord;
rejoicing in hope, preserving in tribulation,
devoted to prayer, contributing to the needs
of the saints, practicing hospitality.

ROMANS 12:9–13

The characteristics of a woman possessing a hostess' heart were modeled by my mother. She could, and often did, invite someone home from church because she had not only prepared a tasty meal for her family, but also had enough extra to include others. I grew up "helping in the kitchen" as a young child. Later, as my mother's health failed, I assumed much of the food preparation responsibilities under her supervision. When I enrolled in college and chose Home Economics as my major, I realized that I had learned many food preparation skills at home; my college classes helped me align the academic principles with my existing skills.

Regrettably, too many Christian young women do not enjoy the type of Titus 2:3–5 relationship that I experienced with my mother—in fact, in twenty-first-century society such an experience is the exception rather than the rule. The first time that we offered our Meal Management class at the college, we found that our students' concept of "home cooked" differed greatly from ours. Lisa carefully taught the students the menu planning process (see chapter seven of *Becoming a Woman Who Pleases God*) and approved their menus before they shopped. What appeared on paper to be a "home-cooked" meal was, in reality, a collection of precooked items that were simply "assembled at home." While we all choose to use convenience foods from time to time, as good stewards of our resources and guardians of our bodies (that are literally temples of the Holy Spirit according to 1 Corinthians 3:16–17), it is important that we know how to practice having a hostess' heart without the aid of a "commercial maid." Knowing these skills allows the use of convenience foods to be a management decision rather than a necessity; in that way the Wise Woman has the opportunity to weigh all of God's principles in her decisions and prioritize them by God's values.

This past summer I attended a wedding shower for one of our students. "Name the Cake" was one of the games, and I had a great time identifying the cakes that went with such questions as "What cake is the biggest flop?" "What cake is found on the ocean floor?" and "What cake is as lovely as a transparent fabric?" As we shared our answers, I was amazed that most of the guests were not familiar with the upside down cake, sponge cake, and chiffon cake. Knowing firsthand what a creative outlet baking can be, I was saddened to realize that many twenty-first-century women have not experienced the fulfillment that comes from mastering a challenging recipe and then sharing it with family and friends. Let's take a look at the motivating force that drives a woman's choice of whether or not to be a hostess—her heart.

WHAT IS THE HEART?

Watch over your heart with all diligence,
For from it flow the springs of life.
PROVERBS 4:23

As Christian women we are concerned with two forms of the heart—the physical heart and the spiritual heart. The physical heart provides nourishment, sustenance, and energy throughout the entire body. If a weakness, either by breakdown or disease, occurs within the heart, it could lead to weaknesses in the rest of the body. The spiritual heart is the center of thinking and reason (Proverbs 3:3; 6:21; 7:3), the emotions (Proverbs 15:15, 30), and the will (Proverbs 11:20; 14:14). What's inside it affects our speech (Proverbs 4:24), sight (Proverbs 4:25), and conduct (Proverbs 4:26–27). The condition of our spiritual heart determines our spiritual health and ultimately controls how we respond to biblical instruction about developing the heart of a hostess. Proverbs teaches us that we have either a wicked and foolish heart or a righteous and wise heart. The wicked and foolish heart despises correction (Proverbs 5:12), is proud (Proverbs 14:14; 18:2, 12), lacks discretion (Proverbs 12:23; 19:3), and is hard (Proverbs 28:14). Standing in stark contrast is the righteous and wise heart that receives commands (Proverbs 10:8), has wisdom and understanding (Proverbs 14:33), seeks knowledge (Proverbs 15:14), and learns and grows (Proverbs 16:23). Which type of heart do you have?

RESPONDING TO THE BIBLICAL
TEACHING ABOUT HOSPITALITY

Do not neglect to show hospitality to strangers,
for by this some have entertained angels without knowing it.
HEBREWS 13:2

Since the Bible is clear that Christians ought to extend hospitality, let's look at how the woman with a wise heart responds to the biblical teaching about hospitality. We will first use the letters that form the word HOSTESS as our guide and build upon a foundation of Scripture by providing some practical tips to prompt us to become "doers of the word, and not merely hearers" (James 1:22–25).

H HOME is the arena where we practice hospitality. While it is fun to eat in a restaurant, our homes should be the environment that allows us to minister to the hearts of others in a more intimate and less structured way than we can when we are in a public environment. Several years ago, we asked our college president's wife, Patricia MacArthur, to speak to our students in the Family Living class. She responded by inviting our students to her home for breakfast because she felt that she could best communicate her heart in her own environment. Our students returned from the tasty breakfast and delightful morning with a vivid picture of what a hospitable home and the heart of a hostess look like. She might have spoken the same words from a classroom podium; however, her impact on the students was magnified because she chose to take the time to entertain them in her home.

John 14:2 teaches us that a heavenly home is being prepared for us. Similarly, our earthly homes should be prepared for those who belong there. Titus 2:3–5 reminds us that women are directed to maintain a godly home; it is important to remember that this passage is not a suggestion—it's a mandate! Proverbs 31:27 describes the noble woman as one who looks well to the ways of her household, while Matthew 5:14–16 challenges us to spiritually construct our lives (and that includes our homes) so that they are like "a city set on a hill," providing others with a visual example of how to practically live the Christian life. How does your family view your home? Let me encourage you to put your book aside for a moment, walk to the outside of the front door, close it, and then open it. Form a "first impression" of what your family sees when they return home. If it is not a "prepared place," what modifications will you make so that it is? How can you make this a family project rather than totally your responsibility?

O OPEN is the attitude of our hearts in offering hospitality to others. Acts 10:34, Romans 2:11, and Galatians 2:6 all remind us that our Father shows no partiality. As His daughters, we are to model His example and be willing to entertain a variety of people. Matthew 5:43–48 teaches us that we are to demonstrate love to our neighbors—both to those who love us and those who hate us. Luke 14:12–14 instructs us to invite the needy, who probably will never be able to repay us, and James 2:1–10 warns us that if we choose to continually show favoritism to certain people, we are sinning.

While Lisa and Mark regularly extended hospitality while they lived in an apartment, when God provided the means for them to purchase their first home, one of the first things that Lisa shared with me was her desire that it would accommodate Mark's entire staff (you'll learn in chapter eight that some modifications were necessary before the first invitation was extended). I am continually blessed to see how many different people the Tatlocks entertain—guests who were invited in advance and last-minuters eat meals at their table and enjoy the comfort of the "Tatlock Bed and Breakfast." Their children are growing up with a clear picture of what it means to have an open home. How open is your home and how diversified are your guest lists? Try setting a goal of hosting at least one social occasion a month that challenges you to leave your "entertaining comfort zone."

S SUBMISSIVE describes a person who responds to God's instruction with a joyful spirit. In his comments on Romans 12:9–13, John MacArthur urges us to not merely entertain our friends but to "pursue the love of strangers" through hospitality.[1] Titus 1:5–8 directs church leaders to teach hospitality by personal example. Hebrews 13:2 is a reminder that one never knows the far-reaching results of extending hospitality, while 1 Peter 4:9 is a description of the kind of attitude of the heart that is to accompany our extension of hospitality. As you consider the truth of these Scriptures, evaluate your attitude in relation to entertaining those you would regard as "strangers." Does the result of your evaluation reveal a heart that is submissive or resistant to our heavenly Father's hospitality instructions? As a family, meditate on these Scriptures and develop a plan for including "strangers" on your guest lists—even if in the beginning it is a bit awkward.

T TEACHER and TEACHABLE. To be able to share knowledge with others, a woman needs to be able to receive instruction as well.[2] Titus 2:3–5 portrays the older woman's skill and godliness that give her the right and credibility to instruct the younger women in the church. Two important implications emerge from this passage: older women are to be willing to share their wisdom and the younger women are to be willing to receive it. Ruth 3:18 is a beautiful example of a younger woman receiving instruction from an older woman—and her mother-in-law, nonetheless! Are you a wise mother-in-law whom your daughter-in-law wants to learn from?

Are you willing to teach? As a daughter-in-law, do you have a teachable spirit? Remember that Proverbs coaches us that "fools despise wisdom and instruction" (Proverbs 1:7). If you are a younger woman, identify a godly woman and ask her to allow you to spend several hours with her; if your age is considered "mature," either physically or spiritually, demonstrate an availability to be an "older woman" in a "younger woman's" life.

Several years ago I was asked to present a series of seminars at a large denomination's women's retreat. I was excited to have the opportunity to share biblical truths and meet new ladies. As I stood before the assembly, I was impressed to see how many chronologically older women were in attendance. My first reaction was, *I hope that when I am the age of some of these ladies I am still teachable.* However, as I thought about the audience later in the evening, I realized that there was an absence of younger women in the group. My joy at the teachability of these older saints diminished as I questioned whether or not they were willing to expand their relational borders and invite younger women to come attend with them. Many times the younger woman simply needs the invitation of an older woman who "knows the ropes." Other times she may need some financial assistance. There is also the possibility that she needs someone to attend to her family responsibilities so she can participate. An older woman can encourage the younger woman in any of these areas —extending the invitation, inviting her as a guest, providing the funds for a sitter, or perhaps staying home herself and attending to the family responsibilities so the younger woman can attend the event. You are an older woman to someone— what can you do to encourage the younger woman in her faith?

My friend Liz writes and speaks about the concept that homemaking can be learned. She shares that "effective housekeeping isn't one of the many spiritual blessings we receive immediately and automatically when we become Christians. But the how-to's of homemaking can be learned, and Scripture says that the older women in the faith are to teach younger women these how-to's."[3] She offers a poignant description of how a woman she admired invited her into her home to provide Liz with the initial direction and nudge for her to tackle the task of effective homemaking; it is a source of encouragement for both younger and older women. What was true in Liz's life in relation to her homemaking skills is the same for anyone needing a model to develop the heart of a hostess. If you lack the skills to get started, won't you pray that our Lord will lead you to a "hospitality mentor"? I am sure that, like Liz's "homemaking mentor," your "hospitality mentor" will be delighted to share her how-to's with you!

E   ENCOURAGEMENT. The attitude and words of the hostess are to inspire her guests. Proverbs 25:11 and 15:23 provide an artistic description of well-chosen words. First Timothy 3:11 reminds us that women in leadership are to refrain from gossip, and Galatians 6:10 is a reminder that our love for fellow Christians is the primary test of our love for God.

Romans 12:15 teaches us that we are to be glad in the blessings, honor, and welfare of others—no matter what one's own situation, and to be sensitive or compassionate to the hardships and sorrows of others. We know from our study of the Wise Woman in Proverbs that wise speech is characteristic of her conversations (31:26), while James 1:26 is a reminder that our conversations reveal the purity of our hearts. Make a concentrated endeavor to monitor your conversations to ensure that they will be an encouragement to others. Before you speak ask yourself four questions:

- Is it kind?
- Is it true?
- Is it necessary?
- Is it gossip (sharing private information with individuals who are neither part of the problem or the solution)?[4]

S SERENE means calm, peaceful, or tranquil.[5] Many families are less than happy when the lady of the house extends hospitality because she is such a wreck before the occasion occurs. Often her lack of organization and unwillingness to involve others in the planning and preparation process encumbers her with an unnecessary burden.

One warm, fall day several years ago, my friend Karen invited me to her home for lunch. Though I planned to leave campus well in advance of the time I was to arrive at her home, several challenges arose that delayed my departure. I walked out of my office with the prayer on my lips that the traffic flow would allow me to arrive on time (my heavenly Father graciously responded with a "yes!"). Her home was a prepared place for me—the dining room table tastefully set and the environment cool. Her heart was prepared for me as well; her peaceful countenance and calm final preparation of the luncheon made our time together an oasis in the midst of a demanding day. As I returned to campus rested and refreshed, I reflected on how differently I would have felt had she been frenzied and unorganized!

Philippians 4:6–7 teaches us that fret and worry

indicate a lack of trust in God's wisdom, sovereignty, or power. Matthew 6:25–34 is a reminder that our heavenly Father has everything under control—we simply must acknowledge and act upon that truth. First Peter 5:6–7 paints a word portrait of our loving heavenly Father inviting us to transfer all of our stress to Him! As you contemplate how you might cultivate a serene strategy for hospitality, begin by purposing to delight yourself in the Lord and meditate on His Word. You will find that it's a great antidote to anxiety (Psalm 1:2). Then develop strategies that will make entertaining a delight rather than drudgery!

S SPONTANEOUS literally means acting without effort or premeditation.[6] When we cultivate the heart of a hostess we choose to practice John 10:10 with zest and vigor as we purpose to live an abundant life. If we are focused on living the abundant life, we must be willing to let others into "our own little world." That will be more difficult for those whose personalities are more introverted; however, if we choose to keep our world narrow, we will miss many blessings!

Nehemiah 8:10 is a reminder that the joy of our Lord is our strength. Purpose to allow our Lord to develop the heart of a hostess in you. The joy you experience from being obedient to His Word will provide you with the motivation to keep going when you have no strength of your own. First Peter 3:15 reminds us that a godly woman understands what she believes, why she is a Christian, and is able to clearly tell others about her faith. If someone asked you today how you were adopted into God's family, would you be able to concisely tell him or her? Try writing out your testimony and review it until you can communicate it to someone else without notes.

GETTING STARTED

Brethren, I do not regard myself as having
laid hold of it yet; but one thing I do:
forgetting what lies behind and
reaching forward to what lies ahead,
I press on toward the goal for the prize
of the upward call of God in Christ Jesus.
PHILIPPIANS 3:13–14

The attitude of the apostle Paul is one that all women who desire to cultivate the heart of a hostess must embrace. As we study the scriptural passages that challenge us to practice hospitality, most of us can reflect on a time when we tried to extend friendship to others and were met with rejection. If you are like me, Satan can use that rejection as a roadblock to prevent me from obeying my heavenly Father on future occasions. In the verses above, Paul teaches us that he moved toward his heavenly Father's will for his life—that of Christlikeness. He refused to dwell on the past or to drink of the cup of self-pity but, rather, kept climbing higher toward his goal of Christlikeness all the days of his life. If we are to cultivate the heart of a hostess, we must refuse to rely on past virtuous deeds and achievements or to dwell on sins and failures. As well, we must lay aside past grudges and rejection experiences. Instead, we will follow Paul's example and continue the ascent to the top of the "hostessing mountain." That ascent begins with developing proper climbing strategies. Here are some to get you started:

- *Collect and file* simple, inexpensive recipes for desserts and meals.
- *Make a list of people* who would be encouraged by your offer of hospitality—purpose to invite your first guests soon!

- *Start simple*—spontaneously inviting someone home after Sunday evening church is a great beginning.
- *Pray* that our loving heavenly Father will give you joy in demonstrating hospitality to others.
- *Remember* that memories require time and energy to create.
- *Purpose* to nurture a hostess' heart that sincerely communicates "come back soon."
- *Meditate* upon "The Heart of the Christian Hostess," modeled after the format of 1 Corinthians 13, found at the conclusion of this chapter.

A FINAL THOUGHT . . .

As you can imagine, I have received many shower and wedding invitations from my students. As I shopped for appropriate gifts, I always looked for ones that would reflect the training they received in our department, but I was never successful in locating one that would remind them of their Home Economics heritage. While browsing through a cookbook as a potential gift, I realized that many of the recipes begin with convenience foods (which always cost more) rather than basic ingredients. Standing there in the bookstore, God gave me an idea that would allow me to reinforce the students' Home Economics heritage. I could compile a cookbook for them! Thus the birth of *One Step Beyond Lasagna*. I prepare an inscription to each new bride before it is bound, which personalizes the volume for her. The many loving thank-you notes I've received have made the work involved in developing the gift well worth the effort. Recently one of our graduates and her husband relocated to Mexico to serve our Lord in a church-planting ministry. Robin's e-mail to me shortly after they were settled reminded me of the role that I have as an older woman to cultivate the heart of a hostess in a younger woman:

"I just received my cookbooks from California and made your Vera Cruz tomatoes and the Twice-Baked Potatoes! Your recipes are always winners with everyone who tries them. Thank you for your kindness in giving me *One Step Beyond Lasagna* for a wedding present. It is very practical, special, and well-used."

How might you package your skills and knowledge to cultivate the heart of a hostess in others?

THE HEART OF THE CHRISTIAN HOSTESS

If I am a Christian woman who teaches other women about their biblical responsibility to practice hospitality but lack the motivation to apply the teachings to my life, I am arrogant (1 Corinthians 13:3–4).

And though I know about the women of the Bible who practiced hospitality, if I fail to emulate their model, I am nothing (1 Corinthians 10:11).

If I pursue Christian ministry and stay up all night preparing a theologically correct Bible study but fail to open my home to others, I am neglecting the New Testament commands to pursue hospitality (Romans 12:13).

A Christian hostess is gracious (Proverbs 11:16) even when others are not.

She believes that the biblical instructions to pursue hospitality are as relevant today as the day they were written and seeks to integrate them into her daily life. Her home is "a prepared place" for her family, friends, and strangers (John 14:2).

A Christian hostess gleans insight from God's Word that motivates her to develop an open heart to entertaining a variety of kinds of guests (Romans 2:11), a tongue that speaks wisdom and kindness to them (Proverbs 31:26), and a submissive spirit that provides hospitality without grumbling (1 Peter 4:9).

She takes seriously the mandate of Titus 2:3-5 and intentionally acquires instruction in time management, family finance, nutrition, food preparation, and the art of hospitality so that God's Word is not discredited.

As for professional contacts, they will diminish in importance; as for speaking opportunities, they will be presented and the content forgotten; as for strategic social events, they will occur and the memories will fade; but the woman who develops the heart of a hostess will be blessed because she chose to fulfill the New Testament commands to practice hospitality (3 John 8, 1 Timothy 3:1-2 and Titus 1:7-8).

So, both the Christian woman and the Christian woman who has the heart of a hostess abide in the Christian community; however, the Christian woman who has the heart of a hostess cultivates a lifestyle that reflects her values and a character that aligns with the Word of God.

GROWING IN THE
ABILITY TO CULTIVATE
A HOSTESS' HEART

1. *Evaluate your heart condition in relation to biblical hospitality.*

    a.   *Write down several personal goals that will help you cultivate a hostess' heart.*

    b.   *Pray that our loving heavenly Father will give you joy in demonstrating hospitality to others.*

    c.   *Record your growth as you cultivate a hostess' heart.*

2. *Write out your testimony and review it until you can communicate it to someone else without notes. Mark your Bible with the path of salvation: Romans 3:10, 3:23, 5:8, 5:12, 6:23, 10:9, 10:10, and 10:13.*

3. *Review chapter ten: "The Wise Woman Practices the Titus Two Principle" in* Becoming a Woman Who Pleases God.

    a.   *Identify a godly "older woman," and ask her to allow you to spend several hours with her. As you write your thank-you note to her, review what you learned from your time together.*

    b.   *Demonstrate the availability to be an "older woman" in a "younger woman's life." Meditate on what you learned from your interactions*

*with an "older woman," and then develop sev-
eral ideas that would help cultivate a relationship with a younger woman.*

4. *Purpose to delight in the Lord and meditate on His
Word. This is a great antidote to anxiety (Psalm 1:2). Then
develop strategies that will make entertaining a delight
rather than drudgery!*

5. *Evaluate your attitude in relation to entertaining those
you would consider "strangers." As a family, meditate on
these Scriptures and develop a plan for including
"strangers" on your guest lists.*

*S*everal years ago my husband and I were able to purchase our first home. I remember the day that we found our house as vividly as if it were yesterday. Our realtor had spent most of the morning showing us homes in our area. It had been rather discouraging because there were few homes available that were also within our budget. We had prayed for many years that the Lord would allow us to have a home where we could expand our ministry to family and friends. Our realtor had one last home to show us that had recently appeared on the market.

We drove down the street through an older, well-kept neighborhood to the last house on the corner. The yard was not in very good condition, but the house itself looked like it was in good shape. We continued through the front door and proceeded to look around. After viewing each room, the realtor asked, "So, what do you think?" My husband responded with enthusiasm and excitement, "It's great! It's perfect!" He went on to list all of the positive features of the home, the fireplace, the large rooms, the kitchen size, the open living room, the location, the view, the parking for large groups, and much more! He was thrilled!

My response to the house was quite different. It was as if we had walked through two entirely different houses! As we entered the home, I saw the worn two-tone grey, shag carpet (that smelled like the little dog that lived there), walls that needed patching and paint, and a gold, bottle glass window on the stair landing that reflected its amber light throughout the house making it seem dark and gloomy. I saw the mismatched door handles, broken light fixtures, and holes in the vinyl floors. In addition to the obvious repairs that needed to be made, there were numerous cosmetic issues to address, like the mirrored, square tiles that had been randomly glued to the closet doors, the hospital-like blue paint throughout the house, the avocado-green stove that contrasted nicely with the gold dishwasher, and the oversized, round, charcoal-grey globe lights in the hallways. I was definitely NOT excited about this house!

Later that evening, my husband and I were talking and praying about the house. I began to realize that my husband had viewed the house for its potential and was not really impacted by its current condition. I, on the other hand, had only seen a house that needed numerous repairs, replacement parts, and lots of cleaning! My husband is a man of vision, and he believed that the house could be made into a warm and inviting home for our family. He was excited about the possibility of "fixing up" the house.

Following the leadership of my husband, who was convinced that

God had heard our prayers and provided the perfect house, I agreed that we should proceed in faith and purchase it. Over the next several years, we slowly made the needed house repairs, including replacing flooring, door handles, and light fixtures. We painted every surface in the house that could possibly be painted! Our home has gradually been transformed into a comfortable, warm, and functional dwelling for our family. While there is still much work to be completed to continue to bring the house into good working order, there were many lessons from this first house-buying experience.

I have learned, from my husband, not to always view things as they are, but to view them as they could be. I have learned how much work it takes to maintain and organize a house. However, the work is well worth the effort, and working to build a home instills in your heart an appreciation for your home. I have gained knowledge in the use of colors, styles, and design principles as we worked to decorate each room in our house. I have found that working together with my husband to build a house into a home creates precious memories that are more valuable than any material thing. Most importantly, I have learned that God intended for us to be creative beings, just as He modeled for us with His own creation. I have reflected on the fact that God was the Original Designer and that . . .

EIGHT

THE WISE WOMAN CREATES A BEAUTIFUL HOME

*God saw all that He had made,
and behold, it was very good.*
GENESIS 1:31

How do I make a house into a beautiful home? Before we can answer this question we ought to define *beautiful*: "very pleasing to see or hear; delighting the mind or senses."[1] Beauty is often experienced or defined through the use of our senses; for example, the enjoyment we experience from *seeing* an exquisite painting, *smelling* a fresh-cut flower, or *hearing* music we enjoy. Beauty, therefore, is what we each define as aesthetically pleasing to see, hear, smell, taste, or touch. This makes the definition of *beautiful* a very individual opinion. This chapter will provide suggestions for creating a beautiful interior; however, your distinct views on what you consider to be aesthetically pleasing will determine how you implement these principles.

Before going further in this chapter it is also important to remind ourselves that we all have unique life circumstances and individual abilities that must be considered when applying interior design principles. For example, we each have unique budget constraints, family characteristics (like the number of children that we have and health conditions), ministry commitments, and many other priorities that may take precedence over implementing these design concepts.

We have previously discussed principles related to budgeting, stewardship, home management, personal priorities, decision-making skills, time management, and numerous other topics related to our character as Christian women.[2] Most of these other areas ought to be addressed before we spend much time focusing on the decorating of our homes.

The motivation for this chapter is to encourage you to view the work of beautifying your home as part of building a warm and welcoming place for your family and friends. Just as cleaning your house or washing dirty laundry communicates your love for your family, so can the attention you give to decorating. The concepts presented in this chapter are just tools and should be implemented only if biblical priorities are maintained in regard to your time, relationships, energy, and resources.

GOD THE CREATOR

In the beginning God created the heavens and the earth.
GENESIS 1:1

The ability to enjoy beautiful things is a precious gift from God our Creator. God planned for His creation to be both beautiful and enjoyed as beautiful. Genesis 2:9 states, "Out of the ground the Lord God caused to grow every tree that is pleasing to the sight . . ." God is the original designer of beauty.

Examples of God's beauty are seen in His creation of color, His variety in form, and His creativity in design. In Edith Schaeffer's book *The Hidden Art of Homemaking*, she describes God as

> the only artist who is perfect in all forms of creativity—in technique, in originality, in knowledge of the past and future, in versatility, in having perfect content to express as well as perfect expression of content, in having perfect truth to express as well as perfect expression of truth, in communicating perfectly the wonders of all that exists as well as something about Himself, is of course God—the God who is personal. God, the Artist![3]

God could have created a black and white world but instead He chose to create a world full of color, textures, and contrasts (such as light and dark). Furthermore, God created humans to enjoy the beauty of His creation by giving them the ability to touch, hear, smell, see, and taste. As John Calvin expressed:

> Has the Lord clothed the flowers with the great beauty that greets our eyes and the sweetness of smell that is wafted upon our nostrils, and yet it is not permissible for our eyes to be pleased by that beauty, or our sense of smell by the sweetness of odor? Did the Lord not distinguish colors, making some more lovely than others? Did he not endow gold and silver, ivory and marble, with a loveliness that renders them more precious than other metals or stones? Did he not, in short, render many things attractive to us, apart from their utility?[4]

It has been said about beauty: "God has implanted in you and in me the capacity to recognize and respond to the beautiful and to derive pleasure from it. The beautiful and our enjoyment of it are among His good gifts to humankind."[5]

All things that bring us enjoyment are gifts from God, because as Christians we acknowledge that all things are *from* God. Ecclesiastes 5:18–19 and 1 Timothy 6:17 remind us the pleasures derived from eating food, the satisfaction from our ability to work, or the accumulation of wealth or possessions are *all* gifts from God. All good things are from God, including the ability to be able to enjoy beauty.

Beauty, as seen in Scripture, not only refers to appreciating aesthetic beauty (like physical attractiveness), but it also refers to an individual's character (1 Peter 3:3–5), kind or good words (Proverbs 15:26; 16:24), and, ultimately, the Lord, Himself (Psalm 27:4; 90:17). Appreciating the beauty of God's creation and understanding that He created us with the ability to value that which is beautiful is important because it helps us to see a glimpse into God's character. God's beauty conveys the idea of a God that is full of grace and favor. As we build a beautiful home, we are reflecting that God has created us as human beings who can appreciate aesthetically beautiful things. But more importantly, as we build our home, we should be reflecting the beauty of the Lord, in other words, reflecting our Creator and His character (Genesis 1:27). Our homes can be beautiful sanctuaries, which reflect that we are people who have been blessed by God's favor and grace through salvation. How do we reflect God's beauty in our homes? For the Wise Woman, it is not through merely decorating with exquisite furnishings or using creative design techniques, but rather, it is through the development of Christlike character. Our character will be reflected in the environment of our homes; as Christians, these homes ought to be full of peace, harmony, order, and grace.

Our homes should reflect *peace* because we have a relationship with God (Romans 5:1; 1 Corinthians 14:33; 1 Thessalonians 5:23). Our homes should be *harmonious* because as Christians we also have the ability to have loving relationships with others who live in or visit our homes (Hebrews 12:14;

2 Timothy 2:22). We members of God's family can live together in unity because of our relationship with God (Ephesians 2:14–17). Peaceful and harmonious homes also require *order* (1 Corinthians 14:33; Colossians 2:5). Order simply means that there are thoughtful or organized procedures that help to maintain peace and harmony in the home. Finally, our homes should be *gracious* (Hebrews 4:16). God's grace was extended to us; therefore, we can create homes that extend grace toward others.

As we begin to discuss basic design principles, we must remember that while we could have the finest home in our neighborhood, we would still not have a *truly* beautiful home if the resulting environment did not also reflect the beauty of the Lord. The beauty we create in our homes will fade with time. However, the beauty of the Lord, which we reflect through our character, will last forever (1 Peter 3:3–5).

UNDERSTANDING BASIC DESIGN PRINCIPLES AND ELEMENTS

By wisdom a house is built,
And by understanding it is established;
And by knowledge the rooms are filled
With all precious and pleasant riches.
PROVERBS 24:3–4

So, how do we begin to "build" our house and "fill" it with precious and pleasant riches? First and foremost, we build our lives upon the solid rock of Christ (Psalm 18:2; 31:3). Through Him, our lives are able to be filled with increasing wisdom and knowledge (Psalm 111:10; Proverbs 1:7; 9:10). As we daily seek Him first and let Him live through us, then we can begin to think about designing living spaces that are pleasing to the eye.

A helpful place to begin when learning about how to create beautiful interiors is to study and understand basic line and design concepts. While some people seem to be born with "good aesthetic judgment," most of us, including myself, need some help getting started. Do you ever spend time looking through home-decorating magazines? Do you ever wonder how interior designers create unique and attractive rooms? The secret of professional interior designers is knowing how to apply line and design principles. They are guidelines that can help you make good aesthetic decisions to create the look and style that you enjoy in your home.

These interior design concepts are typically divided into two categories: design elements and design principles. We will first define terms and then give examples for application of the design concepts in your home.

DESIGN ELEMENTS

The heavens are telling of the glory of God;
And their expanse is declaring the work of His hands.
PSALM 19:1

Design elements include *space, line, shape, color, light, texture,* and *pattern.* The elements of design are the "tools" you have to work with to create a pleasing home environment. Just as an artist uses her paints, brush, and canvas to create a beautiful painting, the interior designer uses space, line, shape, color, light, texture, and pattern to create beautiful interiors.

1. SPACE is simply the enclosed area you are working within. Look at the walls of the room and the space is defined. This is the background for creating your design. Just as an artist is limited to the space of the canvas, so the designer is limited by the defined space. Space should consider aesthetics (arranging furniture in an attractive manner) and function (allowing for comfortable walking traffic patterns).

2. LINE gives direction to a design. Lines have the ability to create a sense of movement in a room, give meaning, and can make a room feel larger or smaller, balanced or unbalanced. The human eye is easily tricked, thinking it sees one thing when in reality it is merely an "illusion." It is important to look at rooms through the lens of "lines." Lines can create visual illusions in your rooms making them appear larger, smaller, or more interesting. There are four basic types of *lines* you will see in your rooms.

- *Vertical lines* add height to a room (columns, vertical blinds, or tall furniture).
- *Horizontal lines* add width to a room (bookshelves or long sofas).
- *Diagonal lines* suggest activity (staircases or slanted ceilings).
- *Curved lines* have a softening effect in a room (rounded door archway or round swags over a window).

3. SHAPE describes how objects *look* (their height, width, or particular lines that create their outline). A well-designed room will use objects with a variety of shapes (e.g., squares, rectangles, or circles).

4. COLOR is one of the first elements of design you notice in a room and is often considered the most important element. Color sets the tone or mood of the room. It has the ability to create a warm, peaceful environment or a busy, stimulating environment.

Colors are often divided into two groupings—warm and cool. Warm colors are the red, orange, and yellow hues. Warm colors are generally considered happy, energetic, and stimulating colors. They tend to feel like they are coming toward you and will often make spaces both appear and feel smaller. The cool colors are the blue, purple, and green hues. Cool colors are considered relaxing, soothing, and comfortable.

5. LIGHT is seen in both natural and artificial forms in a room (e.g., sunlight through windows and lamps or ceiling lights). The use of light in interiors is both functional and decorative. It needs to be functional so tasks can be accomplished in the room (for example, lighting for reading). Lighting is also a powerful decorative element of design that adds interest to a room, can change the ambiance of a room, or even emphasize a focal point of a room. Lighting is often overlooked by beginner designers and is an important element to consider when creating beautiful interiors.

6. TEXTURE simply refers to the way the surface of something feels and looks. It appeals to both the senses of touch and sight and can be seen or felt in rooms, according to the roughness or smoothness of the objects placed in it. Texture adds interest to a room and will make the colors in it look darker or lighter (e.g., smooth textures look larger and lighter, rough textures look smaller and darker). A well-designed room uses a variety of textures.

7. PATTERN is decorative design. It is seen in fabrics, wallpaper, or flooring. Too much use of a pattern in a room makes the room look "too busy" and is not comfortable. Patterns in rooms should be related through the use of color, texture, or a motif that ties them together. There should only be one bold pattern in each room. Once the dominant pattern has been established, the use of smaller, more subdued patterns should be used to complement the dominant pattern.

DESIGN PRINCIPLES

The hearing ear and the seeing eye,
The Lord has made both of them.
PROVERBS 20:12

Design *elements* are the "tools" to be used to create beautiful interiors; in contrast to this, design *principles* are "rules" to follow when decorating that generally will lead to creating pleasing interiors. They are professionally established guidelines that help create aesthetically pleasing interiors. Design principles include *scale and proportion, balance, rhythm, emphasis,* and *harmony.*

1. SCALE and PROPORTION describe the overall size of objects in the room compared to other features of the room (space, furniture, or architectural features). The design goal is to have a complimentary scale for everything in a room. For example, the furniture, the accessories (like a mirror on the wall), and the overall size of the room itself should be complementary. A small chair next to a large sofa looks even smaller. Large furniture looks even larger in a small room.

2. BALANCE gives symmetry and stability to a room. There are two common types of balance used in designs—formal and informal. We can illustrate the two types of balance by thinking of a plain fireplace mantel with an imaginary line down the center:

   • *Formal balance* on the mantel would occur when the objects on either side of the mantel are exactly the same. For example, identical topiary trees placed on either end of the mantel.

- *Informal balance* on the mantel occurs when the objects differ on either end of the mantel in size, shape, and color, but maintain the equilibrium (or balance) for each side. For example, the left side of the mantel might still have one tall topiary tree with a grouping of books and the right side of the mantel might display a round plate next to a tall birdhouse.

The principle of balance can be applied to decorating rooms in a number of different ways. For example, it can be applied to how furniture is arranged on opposite sides of the room, to wall arrangements, or to the placement of objects on a bookshelf. Balance is always critical to consider in any "arrangement" of objects or furnishings.

3. RHYTHM has to do with how the eye moves from one area of the room to another. Rhythm can be accomplished by repeating elements, such as the color or texture of the fabrics. It can also be introduced by repeating a pattern or shape in a room (e.g., hanging three, square picture frames in a row).

4. EMPHASIS is simply creating a focal point in the room. Some rooms have "built-in" focal points such as fireplaces, a beautiful view out a window, or decorative architectural features. Some rooms require that a focal point be added—a large floor rug, works of art on the wall, or large pieces of furniture. Every room should have one dominant focal point. Having too many focal points in a room de-emphasizes all focal points and makes the room feel crowded and not restful.

5. HARMONY is the final design principle. The concept of harmony ensures that all the design elements previously

discussed "fit together" to create a unified room. Harmony suggests that everything in the room blends together comfortably but there is also variety to add interest and keep the room from becoming boring. The elements and principles of design should help you as the designer to accomplish your goals for interior design. Design goals can include:

- Creating a *beautiful* home environment.
- Creating a *functional* home that meets the needs of your family and guests.
- Creating an *economical* budget that stays within the parameters of the family budget.
- Creating an *interesting* but unified home that reflects your unique tastes.
- Creating a *prepared* home to meet the needs of others.

Once we have a basic understanding of design elements and principles, we are ready to move on to discussing practical application ideas for decorating.

CREATIVE AND ECONOMICAL DECORATING FOR STEWARDSHIP

*In this case, moreover, it is required
of stewards that one be found trustworthy.*
1 CORINTHIANS 4:2

As Wise Women, we ought to never forget that we are stewards of everything the Lord has allowed us to possess; this includes both our money and possessions. Another word for steward is "manager." Since we are simply managers of the Lord's resources, we must be careful to make wise decisions regarding how we use those resources. Decorating a home is *not* our highest priority in life. Since we want to avoid materialistic excess as Christians, we need to consider two principles:

1. Always live within our means, and
2. Be creative and thrifty in all our decorating endeavors.

LIVING WITHIN OUR MEANS

Do not store up for yourselves treasures on earth, where moth and rust destroy, and where thieves break in and steal. But store up for yourselves treasures in heaven, where neither moth nor rust destroys, and where thieves do not break in or steal; for where your treasure is, there your heart will be also.
MATTHEW 6:19–21

A Wise Woman acknowledges that she is merely a steward of the resources the Lord has lent to her. Therefore, she will desire to be found faithful in the management of those resources. A Wise Woman who is "fiscally responsible" will establish certain parameters for handling her finances, including the finances for decorating her home. A few basic principles to keep in mind include:

1. ESTABLISH AND USE A BUDGET

A budget is simply a tool that helps us manage our money wisely. It allows us to see how much money we have coming in and going out and is crucial to living within our means. It is important to establish in your budget a category for your interior decorating expenses. If your budget does not allow for money to be spent on "extras," this is probably not the time to be spending *any* money on decorating. It is a time to be content with where the Lord has you financially. Remember 1 Timothy 6:6: "But godliness actually is a means of great gain when accompanied by contentment."

2. Save, Pay Cash, and Avoid Using Credit

I would recommend that you never incur debt for furnishings, accessories, or other items used to decorate your home. Most home furnishings rapidly lose the value of their purchase price and usually do not represent items that will give you a return on your investment. Proverbs 22:7 reminds us that "the borrower becomes the lender's slave." Delaying a purchase to pay cash requires you to be disciplined (as you save each month) and develops your character (self-control and patience). Becoming a woman who shows restraint with her finances will help protect you against materialistic excess.

3. Develop a "Big Picture" Plan for Your Interiors by Thinking Long-term

A practical suggestion that often helps us live within our means is to decide in advance our long-term goals for our interiors (e.g., styles for furniture). This helps protect us from foolishly buying home furnishing on a "whim." You are less likely to make mistakes and waste your resources if you take a thoughtful approach to planning your interiors. An analogy to this is found in Luke 14:28, where Jesus teaches that it is good to "sit down and calculate the cost" of something we are planning to do. This holds true for both building your home and following Christ.

4. Be Content and Use What You Already Own

First Timothy 6:8 states: "If we have food and covering, with these we shall be content." It is easy to get "wrapped up" in the world of designer fashions for interiors. We are told every day that we need more. Scripture says that becoming a lover of money will get us into all kinds of evil (1 Timothy 6:10). A

Wise Woman will practice contentment in her home, remembering her true priorities in life.

5. Maintain a Generous Heart

A Wise Woman will be a *giver,* not an *accumulator* of possessions. If we have taken on debt and stretched our budget so tightly that we have no flexibility to be a giver, we will miss opportunities to meet the needs of others. Once again, we will have misplaced our priorities in life. Acts 20:35 reminds us to "remember the words of the Lord Jesus, that He Himself said, 'It is more blessed to give than to receive.'"

CREATIVE DECORATING TECHNIQUES
*Whatever your hand finds to do,
do it with all your might.*
ECCLESIASTES 9:10

Once the guidelines for your finances have been established most women will find that in order to stay within their budget, they will need to be resourceful and thrifty with their decorating. There are many things you can do to help economically decorate your homes. Those ideas include:

1. Define Your Style

Your home will have a more "put together" look if you take time to develop and know your own personal likes and dislikes. You need to know your style. An easy way to help you discern your individual style is to create an "idea file." Every time you see pictures of styles you like put them in your idea file (for example, collect pictures of furniture, accessories, window treatments, or even the way a particular room *looks*). By creating an idea file you will quickly identify your favorite styles or looks.

This will help guide your decision making as you select your home furnishings and accessories. Your goal is to make all the "pieces" of your decorating create a unified design. Another alternative to defining your style is to simply "replicate" styles you enjoy. Certain styles such as French Provencal, Oriental, or American Country have "pre-determined" looks that can be easily recreated.

2. PAINT IT!

Paint is a wonderful decorating tool—it is both affordable and forgiving; meaning you can always paint it over again if you do not like the product. Paint can be used on fabric, furniture, floors, walls, and ceilings. The possibilities are endless. You do not have to be an "artist" to paint. You simply have to be able to follow the directions. Many painting techniques require only a few simple supplies, which makes painting affordable and easy for even busy women to accomplish. You can go to your local hardware store for the needed supplies and directions to accomplish each procedure.

3. USE COLOR.

Color should be selected based on the atmosphere you desire to create for the room. While there is much that could be said about color, understanding a few simple guidelines will help you select appropriate colors for your interiors; they include:

- Begin by selecting colors you and your family enjoy. The colors that are pleasing to your family are probably the same colors that will create the right atmosphere for your home.
- Light, dull, and cool colors have *receding* qualities that will make rooms appear larger.

- Dark, bright, and warm colors have *advancing* qualities that make rooms appear smaller.
- Using similar colors that blend together creates a restful mood (i.e., using various shades of blue in a room).
- Light impacts color. Colors will look different in artificial and natural light. Artificial light often *softens* colors. Before using fabrics, paint, or other elements of color, you should view the color over twenty-four hours. Mount a swatch of fabric or sample of paint on the wall and observe it throughout the day to see if it is the right choice in the various forms of light.
- Texture changes color. Smooth textures reflect light making them appear lighter and brighter, while rough textures make colors appear darker.
- Color schemes look best if one color dominates and then two or three additional colors are used to complement the main color.
- Contrasting colors draw attention to themselves; for example, a dark sofa against a white wall draws attention to itself. Too many strong contrasts in a room make it tiring, confusing, and often *not* tied together.
- Consider all the elements of the room—furniture, accessories, artwork, etc., when selecting the color scheme. It should complement, not compete with the other elements of the room.
- Don't forget to use neutrals in every room. They help to both blend and tie contrasting hues together. Examples of neutrals include white, cream, black, and brown.
- There are traditional color schemes used by designers such as American Country that uses red, white, and blue or French Provencal that uses yellow and blue. Replicating a color scheme from a picture might be an easy place to start.

4. USE FABRIC

Fabric is often one of the first things noticed in a room. It is part of the color scheme, and its use should be thought through very carefully. Some guidelines include:

- Select one dominant fabric and use it consistently throughout the room; repeat it by using it in pillows, draperies, or upholstered fabrics.
- Use two or three additional fabrics to complement the dominant fabric.
- Mix floral, stripes, plaids, or prints to create interesting combinations; however, make sure they share a common design element (for example, they all have the same color in them somewhere or share the same motif).
- Make sure the fabrics selected complement the desired mood of the room; select formal fabrics for formal rooms, etc.
- Select fabrics that coincide with the decorating style of the room. For example, Modern Contemporary might use black, white, and greys.
- Select fabrics that not only look great but will perform great. Not all fabrics are created equal! Fabrics are made up of various fibers that have different performance characteristics—research before purchasing fabrics.

5. USE TEXTURE

Texture is a design element that is often overlooked. It is important to remember three points:

- *Texture affects color*—rough textures appear darker and smooth textures appear brighter.

- *Texture sets the tone or mood* of the room (for example, *formal* textures include smooth carved wood, decorative trims, velvet or heavy brocade fabrics, and *informal* textures include iron, painted woods, and twill weaves or corduroy fabrics).
- *Texture adds interest* (use a variety of textures in every room).

6. CREATE INTERESTING WALL ARRANGEMENTS

It is usually our tendency to simply take our favorite pictures, get some nails, and mount them in the center of the wall. We think, "great, our walls are decorated!" Making the most of your wall space requires a little more thought than simply hanging a picture. There are a few guidelines to consider that will help your walls look more interesting. You may find you do not have to buy a thing—just use what you already have around the house! To create interesting wall arrangements you can:

- *Identify a focal point.* Select one item, for example a piece of art, a mirror, or a shelf, and build your arrangement around it.
- *Determine the type of balance that you desire.* If you desire to use *formal* balance, you will most easily create it by hanging the same type of objects on the wall (for example, hanging four pictures over a sofa that create a square shape). If you desire to use *informal* balance, you will need to be a little more creative in the type and quantity of items used on each wall. Balance is accomplished when each side of the wall is equally "weighted."
- *Form groupings.* It is usually our tendency to place one object on each wall here and there and be satisfied that our walls are decorated. This style of wall treatment tends

to be boring and uninteresting. While there are locations in homes where placing one object, like a large mirror or piece of artwork, is appropriate, most walls will be more interesting if "groupings" of items have been used.

- *Add dimension to your walls.* Use items that vary in size, shape, and texture as a part of each wall grouping to create depth and dimension. Don't limit your walls to all flat objects. For example, in addition to hanging flat pictures, hang shelves, mirrors, clocks, dried flowers, plates, baskets, quilts, or candlestick holders.
- *Use uneven numbers.* It is a generally accepted rule in decorating that uneven numbers make a more pleasant and interesting composition than even numbers. For example, hanging three pictures in a row versus four. A noted exception to this rule might be seen if you are using formal balance, which often uses evenly dispersed objects to maintain the formality.
- *Avoid clutter.* Don't use everything you have if it does not complement the overall design. Using too much on the wall will make the walls appear disorderly and ultimately *de-emphasizes* the space as the items busily blend into the next item.
- *Know how to arrange your wall groupings*—there are a few guidelines to follow that will help you "pull it all together" when you begin to actually place items on your wall. They include:

  a. *Select the materials in advance for the arrangement.* Identify all of the objects you desire to incorporate in the arrangement. Be sure to consider the style and size of the furniture, the color and style of the surroundings, and the other accessories that will decorate the room. Remember, a muted background lets the pictures dominate.
  b. *Choose the shape of the arrangement.* Consider how

the furniture is placed and then select an appropriate shape for the arrangement. Common shapes for placing the picture or wall objects include: horizontal lines, vertical lines, a cross shape, triangular shape, or "L" shape. Remember to keep the spacing consistent between each picture or object to maintain balance.

c. *Choose the height of the arrangement.* Pictures are generally hung just above eye-level. This will be lower in seating areas (dining rooms) and higher in areas for standing (hallways). Measure down from the ceiling to the top of eye-level and mark with a pencil to give yourself a guideline.

d. *Select the lighting for the arrangement.* Choose subdued lights that will not reflect on glass. Wall lights on either side of the arrangement will add to the atmosphere and create interest. Picture lights will emphasize a particular painting or piece of art and can be used to create a focal point.

e. *Practice first.* Before you actually hang items on the wall, take some time to practice (an easy way to do this is to lay newspaper on the ground in the size of your workspace and arrange the objects until you are satisfied with the shape).

7. DEVELOP YOUR SKILLS

Completing the decorating projects yourself rather than hiring others to complete them will save you money. You may be thinking that you don't have the needed creativity or talent in the area of decorating! I am not an overly "creative" type either, but I can read and follow directions! Usually completing home decorating projects yourself is more about the willingness to try new things rather than how creative you are. So step out, and try something new!

8. ADD A LITTLE LIFE

Plants bring a wonderfully warm feel to any room. Having potted plants, fresh-cut flowers, herbs, or even dried arrangements add life to a room. For a potted plant, select a sturdy one that will thrive in the light and temperature of the room.

9. REMEMBER YOUR "SENSES"

In her book *Creating a SenseSational Home,* Terri Willits suggests that you decorate your home to accommodate all five senses (what you see, smell, hear, taste, and touch).[6] I have found this idea to be a fun and practical suggestion. It helps move me beyond just focusing on the fabrics and colors I am choosing and challenges me to create a warm and inviting environment as a *whole* for my home. Ideas for applying this concept include:

TABLE 8.1 DECORATING WITH THE FIVE SENSES	
Senses	Suggestions
SIGHT	•Area Lighting •Collectibles •Colors (fabrics/paints) •Flowers
HEARING	•Music •Chimes •Bells •Gracious Speech •Waterfalls
SMELL	•Flowers •Potpourri •Candles •Baking •Drawer or Closet Sachets
TASTE	•Bowls of Fruit •Herbs and Spices •Homemade Foods
TOUCH	•Cozy Pillows or Throws •Plush Towels •Comfortable Floor Rugs

10. TASTEFULLY ACCESSORIZE

Accessories refer to the incidental objects placed in the room after the furniture and/or equipment have been arranged. Accessories can be functional (lamps, clocks, or mirrors) or decorative (framed art, flowers, or decorative objects), or sometimes both. Be creative with your accessories. Take some time to look through magazines for examples of items to use. This will help you to be imaginative and avoid being redundant throughout your home. Some guidelines for selecting and placing accessories are:

- Choose accessories that carry the theme or style of the room.
- Use odd numbers (usually considered more pleasing to the eye).
- Less is more! Using too many accessories will clutter the room and usually impact its function (for example, not leaving enough space to set a glass on a table).
- Create groupings of objects. Groupings are usually a more interesting way to display your collectibles (rather than just placing one object here and there). The objects in the groupings should vary in size, shape, and height.

11. PERSONALIZE IT!

We have spent a lot of time talking about general guidelines for decorating your home, but they are just that—*guidelines*. Part of creating a beautiful and inviting home is reflecting your own unique style and personality. Your home should reflect the distinctive characteristics of your family. Displaying family photos is a common way to personalize your home, but beyond this idea we can accessorize with items that reflect our unique family interests, heritage, and life experiences. Other examples include: decorating with books, displaying objects from our individual cultural backgrounds, or hanging pictures depicting your travels. Whatever the means, your home should always reflect the unique individuals God has created who reside there.

CREATING A WARM AND WELCOMING HOME

The wise woman builds her house,
But the foolish tears it down with her own hands.
PROVERBS 14:1

We have discussed both formal and practical principles related to creating beautiful interiors. It would seem that we could now finish our discussion on interior design; however, if we stopped now, we would still be missing several key ingredients to creating a beautiful home. You see, a beautiful home is not just about the fabrics, furniture, or accessories contained within its walls. A beautiful home is also one that is orderly, peaceful, and well-managed. As we conclude our discussion on interiors, it is important to once more acknowledge that exquisite decorating does not necessarily turn a house into a home. A warm and welcoming home is created by remembering that:

• CHARACTER IS CRUCIAL!

A home simply decorated can be a truly beautiful home based on the gracious and loving character of the people residing it in. Likewise, a superbly decorated home can be an uninviting and uncomfortable home if there are contentious, selfish people living there. Colossians 3:12–14 beautifully describes the character of a woman who reflects Christ in her home. This kind of character is essential to building a warm and welcoming home. If I personalize the verses they might read something like this (author's version):

And so, since I have been chosen by God, I will remember that I am holy and beloved, I will put on a heart of compassion, kindness, humility, gentleness, and patience; I will be patient with my family and guests, and whomever I have a complaint against, I will forgive, just as the Lord forgave me. And beyond all these things, I will put on love, which will perfectly bond together my home in unity.

• ORGANIZATION IS ESSENTIAL!

Organization is critical to developing a warm home environment. An organized home is a peaceful and relaxing home. An unorganized home is frenzied and chaotic. A good place to start organizing your home is to first *make sure everything has a place and everything is in its place.* Set yourself up to be successful by first identifying what needs to be organized. Do you need a place to put your mail? Do you need to develop a filing system for your finances? Do you need to organize your children's toys? Do you need to clean out your clothes closet? Start with one project a week until you have organized each area in your home. Second, *remove the clutter* from your home. Put away all the piles that accumulate in your home (you know the ones—piles of mail, magazines, newspapers, craft projects, children's toys, clothes, etc.). Deal with the piles daily by putting everything back into its place at the end of each day.

• CLEANING IS IMPORTANT!

The beauty of our homes will quickly disappear if we do not keep them clean and tidy. A luxurious living room covered in dust is not inviting. A bedroom scattered with clothes on the floor is not comfortable. A sticky kitchen floor ruins the charm and warmth of any décor. Cleaning helps keep our homes both functional and attractive. Titus 2:3–5 admonishes older women to train the younger women to be "workers at home." Keeping a clean home is part of the practical outworking of this principle. Organizing cleaning tasks is the primary challenge of keeping a clean home. A simple way to organize your household cleaning is to create a chart that lists all of your tasks and when they need to be completed (see Table 8.2). Maintaining a *clean* home will help to create an *orderly* home that ultimately contributes to building a *peaceful* home.

• PREFERRING ONE ANOTHER IS VITAL!

A final aspect to consider when creating a warm and welcoming home is to consider the preferences of others. Often as women we feel we have the "right to be in charge of the decorating." This attitude is a violation of the attitude Christ desires for us to have as Wise Women. Christ desires for us to defer to and prefer one another (Romans 12:10). While many men often do not have opinions about the decorating and do completely defer to their wives' decorating tastes, it is important that we do not assume this to be true. We should always seek our husbands' input and invite them to participate in the decorating with us. We are building *their* home (Proverbs 14:1). We should also be careful to build a home that is a comfortable and fun environment for our children. A home that is filled with all "no touches" is stifling. Children should be able to relax, play, and live comfortably in *their* home (make practical as well as beautiful choices in the materials and styles you select for your home).

Finally, we should seek to prepare a welcoming environment for our guests. Our homes should feel like *their* home by our anticipating their needs and seeking to meet them (for example, having comfortable dining, talking, or relaxing areas in our home, depending on the needs of our guests). The principle of *preferring one another* is crucial for us to embrace as we decorate so we build a home that is warm and inviting to others, including our family and friends.

A FINAL THOUGHT . . .

It is important to maintain an eternal perspective in the midst of the fabrics, furnishing, and fun of decorating. Terry Willits provides us with a fitting concluding thought that emphasizes the motivation for the Christian to create a beautiful home when she states:

> The atmosphere we create in our home directly affects our home's most important aspect: the relationships we have there. We want our home to have an atmosphere that allows souls to be replenished, love to flourish, and God to be glorified. Sights, sounds, smells, tastes, and touches are merely a means to minister to our loved ones while here on earth. Furnishings and fabrics will someday be gone. Food will be eaten. Music and laughter will be hushed. Fragrance will no longer fill the rooms. But the memories of the atmosphere and the relationships in our homes will live on forever. I believe the primary reason God has blessed us with our wonderful senses is so that we would stand in awe of Him and be grateful for his goodness to us.[7]

TABLE 8.2
HOUSEHOLD ORGANIZATION & CLEANING SCHEDULE

	Daily	Weekly	Monthly	Quarterly	Semiannually
Family Room	• Pick up piles • Straighten pillows	• Dust • Vacuum	• Vacuum lamp shades • Vacuum upholstered furniture • Clean windows (inside/out)	• Baseboards • Blinds	• Clean floor fans
Kitchen/ Food Preparation	• Scrub sink • Empty/run dishwasher • Wipe countertops • Empty trash • Sweep • Quick mop	• Menu plan • Grocery shop • Wipe out fridge/freezer • Mop floor • Wipe off appliances	• Wash cupboard doors • Wash windows (inside/out) • Clean oven range fan	• Baseboards • Blinds • Clean-out fridge/freezers	• Wash valance • Clean-out pantry
Living Room and Dining Room	• Straighten pillows • Wipe table	• Vacuum • Dust	• Wash stair railing • Clean doors/door handles	• Vacuum baseboards • Clean shutters • Dust chair rail	• Clean light fixtures
Bedrooms	• Make beds • Pick up clothes • Pick up piles	• Change sheets • Vacuum • Dust	• Mirrored closets • Ceiling fan • Vacuum lamp shades	• Vacuum baseboards • Clean blinds • Clean shutters	• Clean floor fans • Turn mattresses • Clean out closets • Check fire alarm batteries
Bathrooms	• Empty trash • Check toilets • Wipe basins	• Showers/tubs • Toilets • Change towels (2–3 times a week) • Mirrors • Mop floors	• Wipe down ceilings • Clean tiles • Shower doors	• Baseboards • Wash curtains	• Clean light fixtures • Wash curtains
Laundry	• Hang/fold clothes • Pretreat stains	• Wash/dry/fold (3 times a week/ M–W–F)	• Dry-cleaning • Mending		• Dry-clean outside coats
Other		• Sweep front entry/ back patio		• Straighten linen closets	• Straighten garage

GROWING IN THE ABILITY TO CREATE A BEAUTIFUL HOME

1. *Identify your motivation for decorating your home.*

   a. *Write a biblical rationale identifying your personal philosophy of interior design. Discuss "why" you desire to have a beautiful home.*
   b. *Consider the principles outlined in this chapter to get you started.*
   c. *Identify at least three key Scriptures that summarize your philosophy.*

2. *Define your style.*
Begin to identify your personal design style by starting your "idea file" as discussed in this chapter. You may want to start several folders for the various categories of interiors (e.g., furniture styles, accessories, color schemes, and/or fabrics).

3. *Evaluate your home in light of the design elements and design principles discussed in this chapter.*

   a. *Identify areas for improvement and ideas for changes to implement each category.*
   b. *Prepare a sample chart like the one below to help you organize your thoughts.*

Design Elements	Ideas for Changes & Implementation	Design Principles	Ideas for Changes & Implementation
Space		Scale & Proportion	
Line		Balance	
Shape		Rhythm	
Color		Emphasis	
Light		Harmony	
Texture			
Pattern			

4. *Establish goals and a savings plan for major interior expenses.*

    a. *Establish a functional family budget before a "decorating budget."*

    b. *Evaluate your budget to determine if there is "extra" for decorating expenses.*

    c. *Identify future expenses for projects or purchases related to your interior decorating and establish a saving plan for each item.*

    d. *Prepare a "goals worksheet" for long-term goals and intermediate goals to help you accomplish your savings goals (see the sample on the next page).*

MAJOR EXPENSES/PURCHASES FOR INTERIOR GOALS
(long-term goals)

GOAL	Cost of goal	Number of years before needed	Amount already saved	Amount to save each year	Amount to save each month
1.					
2.					
3.					
4.					
5.					

MAJOR EXPENSES/PURCHASES FOR INTERIOR GOALS
(intermediate goals)

GOAL	Cost of goal	Month/ date money is needed	Amount already saved	Amount to save each month	Amount to save each pay period
1.					
2.					
3.					
4.					
5.					

5.   *Prepare a* Personal Household Cleaning Chart.

    a.   *Use the sample chart in this chapter and customize it to reflect your own personal cleaning needs.*

    b.   *Once you have tailored the chart to reflect your household, place it in a convenient location for easy reference.*

    c.   *Begin to use it each week or month as a tool to help you improve your household organization.*

One of my favorite memories of growing up was my mom's tradition of making me a new Easter dress. Every spring my mom and I would go shopping to pick out the fabric and supplies for the dress. I would watch her carefully sew each piece together, getting more excited as the weeks grew closer to Easter Sunday. As a child, it helped make Easter Sunday a very special celebration. I can still remember most of the details of each dress my mom sewed for me.

It has been many, many years since my mom has made a dress for me! But I still associate "special clothes" with "special occasions." The clothes we wear on special dates, holidays, or even to business appointments can communicate that the event is important. My family and I still practice this principle on Sundays when we choose to dress nicely because it communicates that we honor God and respect our church. Our clothing helps us separate Sundays from the other days of the week.

While how people dress is not an indicator that their hearts are prepared to worship, it outwardly signifies that church is a special event. I recently had a great reminder of this one Sunday morning. My husband and I arrived at church ready to spend the morning in worship and fellowship. As we took our seats, I looked down at my shoes and discovered that I had two completely different shoes on! I had a black shoe on my right foot and a blue shoe on my left foot! They were obviously different shoes! My first response was one of embarrassment for the careless mistake that I had made while getting ready that morning. My second response was to want to go home immediately and change my shoes (vanity rearing its ugly head)! This, however, was not an option since we have a lengthy drive to church. After a few moments, I gained the courage to show my husband my feet. Immediately, we were both struck with the humor of my wearing two mismatched shoes! As we restrained our laughter, I reflected on my situation. I thought to myself—who really cares what is on my feet? I came that morning to worship God. It did not matter what I was wearing. I had often spent too much time "making sure my shoes matched" and not enough time preparing my heart to worship the true and living God. Just as I spend time selecting appropriate clothes, I need to spend time preparing my heart. Do I confess sin, read God's Word, and praise Him for His goodness in preparation for worship? How easy it is to focus solely on the outward and forget about the inward! As I walked around church all morning with mismatched shoes, it was a good lesson for me that Sunday that a Wise Woman understands the true definition of beauty. She knows that her character is what makes her a beautiful woman in the eyes of the Lord. While we might enjoy wearing the latest fashions . . .

THE WISE WOMAN DRESSES WITH DISCERNMENT

*Strength and dignity are her clothing,
And she smiles at the future.*

PROVERBS 31:25

Clothing provides us with a creative means of expressing our unique personalities. Clothing is one element of our personal communication. It can tell a lot about who we are and what we do in life. The executive woman wearing a business suit, the mommy wearing overalls, and the athlete wearing sports attire all communicate something about who these people are and their life responsibilities. As Christian women, our clothing should do the same thing—it should be a reflection of who we are. The message our outer clothing sends about who we are should be consistent with our inner Christian character.

There are many practical principles that a Wise Woman can

apply to her clothing selection that will allow her to look her best while keeping the focus on her character. We will discuss a few of them later in this chapter. However, before we can discuss the practical guidelines, I think it is important to remind ourselves of why we have clothing in the first place. Reflecting on the origins of clothing helps "put clothes into perspective" for me and helps me gain a better perspective on the role clothes should play in my life as a Christian woman. Understanding the origins of clothing helps to eliminate the temptation to be enamored with the glamour of the fashion industry and keeps me focused on biblical principles for clothing selection.

THE ORIGINS OF CLOTHING

Then the eyes of both of them were opened, and they knew
that they were naked; and they sewed fig leaves together
and made themselves loin coverings.
GENESIS 3:7

The world has devised many theories regarding the origins of clothes. Some say clothes have evolved solely due to the need for protection from physical elements, some say it is due to cultural influences, and others say it is because of our need for individual expression. While clothing might meet the need of providing warmth, reflect our culture, or allow for expressing our individuality, none of these theories accurately reflects the reason we wear clothes; Scripture, not history of clothing, explains why. As we read the account of Adam and Eve in Genesis 3:7–21, we see that they became aware of their nakedness and covered their bodies after they disobeyed and sinned against God's command not to eat from the Tree of the Knowledge of Good and Evil. Clothing was first designed as a result of sin. Adam and Eve attempted to hide their sinful shame by *physically* covering their bodies. Clothing, therefore, can be a daily reminder of our sin. Romans 5:12 reminds us that sin entered into the world through one man and, as a result, all of us are sinners (see also Romans 3:23). Remembering why we have clothes should help prevent us from becoming consumed with empty vanity related to our clothes.

Not only should clothing remind us of our sin, clothing should remind us of our need for a Savior. Genesis 3:21 says, "The Lord God made garments of skin for Adam and his wife, and clothed them." Just as the fig leaves Adam and Eve sewed together for clothes were inadequate for God, so is any attempt we make to deal with our own sin. Scripture is clear, we have a need for a Redeemer, a Savior (Romans 5:18). We cannot cover our own sin. Christ paid the price for our sin (Hebrews 9:27–28). Christ's sacrifice and death on the cross covers our sin before God (1 Corinthians 15:1–4). Christ died to reconcile us (or bring us back) to God (1 Peter 3:18). Christ's death on the cross was an acceptable sacrifice that allows us to have a restored relationship with God (Romans 8:31–39).

Clothes, therefore, become a daily reminder of our sin (Romans 3:11–12) and our need for a Savior (Romans 6:23). If we have placed our faith in Christ as our personal Savior (Ephesians 2:8–9), we can remind ourselves as we daily cover our bodies that our sin is covered by Christ (Romans 6:23). The Wise Woman understands her need for a Savior and allows her clothes to reflect that she has a personal relationship with God through His Son, Jesus Christ.

BIBLICAL PRINCIPLES RELATED TO CLOTHING SELECTION

As a ring of gold in a swine's snout,
So is a beautiful woman who lacks discretion.
PROVERBS 11:22

We can reflect biblical principles in the choices we make regarding the type of clothes we choose to wear. Scripture identifies several principles we can apply to our clothing selection; they include:

- *Clothing is to be modest,* with propriety (or what is proper), and with moderation or not extreme (this is a command for Christian women)—this can be applied to the style of clothes as well as the quantity of clothes I have, both should reflect the principle of "modest" (1 Timothy 2:9–10).
- *The clothes I wear can be beautiful in materials, style, or color.* Another way to state this principle is that my clothes *can* be fashionable. This reflects that I have thoughtfully selected my clothes and desire to look my best (Proverbs 31:13–22).
- *My clothes can reflect quality workmanship* (Proverbs 31:21–25).
- *I should not be overly consumed or worry about my clothes* (Matthew 6:25–34).
- *I should select my clothing with discretion* (meaning showing good judgment, being discreet, and exercising wise caution[1]), knowing that a woman who lacks discretion is like having a "gold ring in a pig's nose" (Proverbs 11:22 NKJV).
- *My clothing should be feminine* and others should be able to discern I am a woman (Deuteronomy 22:5).
- *Character is always emphasized over clothing;* I should not be overly consumed with my outward adornment (1 Peter 3:3–4, see chapter ten for more discussion of this passage.)
- *The clothes I choose to wear should not be a stumbling block or present a temptation to others,* causing them to sin through lust or jealousy (1 Corinthians 10:32).
- *I am a steward of all the resources God has given me,* including my clothes. Therefore, I understand how to care for my clothes, I carefully budget money for clothes for

my family and myself, and I always seek to get the most for my clothing dollar (1 Corinthians 4:2).

- *I should seek to glorify God in all that I do and say,* including the way I dress. This means certain clothing "styles" are not appropriate for Christians because they are associated or identified with lifestyles that do not glorify God (1 Corinthians 10:31).

- *I am called to be sexually pure and sexually exclusive in a marriage relationship.* The way I dress should not suggest otherwise (Ephesians 5:3; Colossians 3:5).

- *I am "in" the world but not "of" the world.* A mature Christian has developed the ability to separate herself from an ungodly society, including in the area of clothing selection when it is contrary to biblical principles. Current trends in fashion are not the final authority in what is acceptable for me to wear as a Christian (Romans 12:1–2).

Summarizing the principles above, we can conclude that Scripture is very concerned that we make thoughtful, discerning choices regarding the clothes we choose to wear. While we all may not choose to wear exactly the same style—we all can exhibit our godly character through our clothing selection by choosing to wear modest, feminine, and moderate styles of clothing (moderate applied here would mean clothing that is not too extreme in any given style, appropriate for Christians, and not offensive to others in our community because we are willing to defer to their preferences out of love).

MODESTY AND THE CHRISTIAN WOMAN

*Likewise, I want women to adorn themselves
with proper clothing, modestly and discreetly,
not with braided hair and gold
or pearls or costly garments,*

but rather by means of good works,
as is proper for women making a claim to godliness.
1 TIMOTHY 2:9–10

While there are many principles in Scripture to consider when selecting clothes, there seems to be one principle that serves as an umbrella for all others—the principle of modesty. If I do not violate the principle of modesty, I generally will not violate the other principles seen in Scripture that we apply to clothing. For example, looking back over a few of the principles from our previous list, modesty:

- Allows me to select what is proper, moderate, and not extreme in style.
- Allows for fashionable clothes—beautiful in style, materials, color, and workmanship.
- Reflects I have implemented discretion in my clothing choices.
- Allows me to reflect biblical femininity (others know I am a woman).
- Allows my character to remain the focus by *not* drawing attention to any specific part of my physical body.
- Prevents me from being a stumbling block to my brothers or sisters in Christ.
- In the quantity of clothes I own helps me practice good stewardship.
- Protects my current and/or potential relationship with my spouse.
- Separates me from an ungodly society.

As you can see, practicing modesty in clothing selection is important because it helps you carry out other principles in Scripture. What exactly does it mean to be modest? Let's look at 1 Timothy 2:9–10 to answer this question. Paul is addressing several doctrinal issues, including the behavior of women in the church. In this passage women are told to *adorn* themselves with *proper clothing.* "Adorn" is from the Greek word *kosmeo,* from which we get our English word "cosmetic."[2] It means "to arrange," "to put in order," or "to make ready." The first lesson we see about dressing modestly is that as Christian women we *do* need to give thought to our appearance. Our appearance should reflect that we have thoughtfully selected our clothes and carefully prepared our outer appearance. The term "proper clothing" communicates that everything about the woman is prepared to worship God, including her *clothes* and *attitudes.* Another way to say this is that the woman is prepared to worship on the outside and the inside. One author puts it this way, "the well-ordering is not of dress and demeanor only, but of the inner life, uttering indeed and expressing itself in the outward conversation."[3] John MacArthur explains this passage by stating:

A woman must arrange herself appropriately to join God's people as they worship. Part of that important preparation involves the outside, the wearing of *proper clothing.* Proper translates *kosmio,* which like *kosmeo,* derives from the noun *kosmos.* *Kosmos* is often translated "world," but it really means "order," or "system." It is the antonym of "chaos." *Katastole* (clothing) encompasses not only the clothing itself, but also the look—the whole demeanor. Women are to come to the corporate worship ready to face the Lord. They must not come in slovenly disarray or personal display because of an unbecoming wardrobe or demeanor. There is a place for lovely clothes that reflect the humble grace of a woman, as evidenced in Proverbs 31:22, "Her clothing is fine linen and purple." Proper adornment on the outside reflects a properly adorned heart.[4]

Paul goes on to identify specific ways women in the church were drawing attention to themselves rather than reflecting the principle discussed above (being prepared to worship the Lord). He mentions braided hair, gold, pearls, and costly garments (1 Timothy 2:9). He is not forbidding these practices or adornments, but simply using them to illustrate how women were drawing others to focus on outer beauty themselves, rather than on the Lord. Women still struggle today with making good choices about what to wear. We may not wear braided hair, gold, or pearls—but we could substitute any form of extreme, indecent, lavish, or expensive fashion from our current society, and we would become just like the women Paul was addressing—women who draw attention to themselves rather than their character, which ought to reflect a humble godliness.

The words "modestly" and "discreetly" further define a Christian woman's attitude toward her clothing (verse 9). *Aidos* is the word used for modestly.[5] It refers to a woman's humility and her concern for others—concern that she would not cause another to sin (and lead them into the temptation of lust because of how she is dressed). "Modestly" indicates that she is very sensitive to the temptations of others—so much so that it impacts how she dresses. She carefully chooses her clothes so she does not become a stumbling block to others (Matthew 18:6–9). The word "discreetly" simply reinforces this concept of being sensitive to how our dressing impacts others. "Discreetly" means "self-control." We need to have self-control over our own sexual passions and self-control so we do not cause another to sin because of our behavior or how we are dressed. The lesson we learn from this is that our personal preference for clothing styles is *secondary* to our concern for others. Fashion *does not* dictate what I choose to wear; my *character* dictates what I wear. In other words, fashion preferences are not wrong as long as they do not compromise our character.

Paul ends this part of his discussion on women by emphasizing that a woman's good works will be what she is known for, rather than her expensive fashions (1 Timothy 2:10). Her "good works" are another indicator of her character. There must be consistency when comparing appearance and character if a woman claims to be godly. Selecting proper clothing allows your godly character to be emphasized rather than your physical body. To summarize, modesty is a command for Christian women so they will draw attention to their Lord rather than to their bodies. Second, modesty is critical for Christian women to embrace because they are members of a special community—the family of God. Christian women dress modestly so they will not become a stumbling block to others; this is more important to a godly woman than being fashionable.

How do we know the specific type of garments that are modest (e.g., how short is too short, how low is too low, how tight is too tight)? There is an element of modesty that is tied to cultural definitions or personal preferences. For example, a hundred years ago it was considered very immodest to reveal ankles and calves! I would encourage you to pray through each of the Scriptures we have discussed and ask the Lord to reveal if there are areas you need to change in your dressing. If your heart is tender and teachable, I am confident the Lord will give you a peace or lack of peace over your clothing choices. Also, you can do the following practical steps to discern what is modest:

1. Ask a *godly* dad, brother, or husband his opinions. Men respond to the visual and are impacted by women's clothing differently; Christian men who love us will be honest with us when we seek their advice. Listen to their counsel.
2. Sit in front of a mirror and observe what others see, for example:

   • Bend over to check how revealing your necklines are;
   • Sit down, then cross your legs to check shorts and skirts;
   • Bend over to see how high your skirt moves up;
   • Look at skirt slits, etc., when you take a big step.

3. Ask yourself what you want men who are *not* your husband to see.

- Are you dressing to maintain your sexual purity?
- Are you visually preserving yourself for your husband?

4. Ask yourself if you are willing to defer your preferences out of love for others, and evaluate why you dress the way you do.

- Do you give priority to being "in style" over biblical principles?
- Do you follow fashion at all costs?
- Have you reviewed Scripture to identify principles related to clothing (as we discussed earlier in the chapter)? Ask God to show you if you are violating any of these principles.

Finally, I would encourage you to "err" on the side of modesty—if there is a potential to becoming a stumbling block to another individual or potential to offend another Christian, avoid the clothing completely. A godly woman defers her preferences (and yes, even rights to wear certain clothes) because she is more concerned about others. This principle is seen in 1 Corinthians 10:23–24, "All things are lawful, but not all things are profitable. All things are lawful, but not all things edify. Let no one seek his own good, but that of his neighbor"—this includes how we dress (for further study of this principle see 1 Corinthians 6:12–20; Galatians 5:13–25; Philippians 2:1–11).

PRINCIPLES OF LINE AND DESIGN
FOR CLOTHING SELECTION

She makes coverings for herself;
Her clothing is fine linen and purple . . .

Strength and dignity are her clothing,
And she smiles at the future.
PROVERBS 31:22 , 25

Does being a modest Christian woman mean we never look our best or are never fashionable? Quite the contrary! Using the Proverbs 31 woman as an example, we see a woman who looked beautiful and fashionable. She used quality materials—fine linen (Proverbs 31:22), as well as fashionable colors—scarlet or purple, the colors of royalty (Proverbs 31:21–22). Taking a thoughtful approach to selecting our clothes can be one way we set ourselves apart from the world. I would like to focus on practical guidelines for selecting clothes that "look good" on your individual figure type. There are no two women designed by God exactly alike. That means my figure assets and figure flaws—or "figure challenges" as we affectionately call them—are not necessarily yours and vice versa! We all need to make individual choices that maximize our figure strengths and camouflage our figure weaknesses.

Our goal in clothing selection is to look our best by selecting clothes that modestly compliment our figure. How do we do this? To select clothes that are flattering to your figure, you have to have a basic understanding of *design principles and elements*. Design principles and elements are the guidelines used by professional clothing designers, they include:

1. USE THE POWER OF *LINES*

Lines in garments can be created by the construction details (seam lines, necklines, or collar shapes) or by applied details (such as a row of buttons or stitching). Lines are powerful because they create *visual illusions*. This simply means that lines can fool our eyes! Since lines "lead" our eyes, they have the potential of making you appear taller, shorter, concealing your

weight, or drawing attention to a particular part of your garment (and, yes, body!). Our eyes naturally follow lines. For
example, our eyes follow the outline of the garment, the depth
of the neckline, or the rise in the slit of a skirt. Selecting appropriate lines for your figure type is important to balance out
figure imperfections. It is equally important to consider lines in
the context of practicing modesty. Here are a few principles
to remember when using lines to flatter your figure:

- *Horizontal lines* lead the eye across the body, adding
  width and making the figure appear shorter and wider.
- *Vertical lines* move the eye up and down adding height and
  making the figure appear taller and more slender.
- *Curved lines* (e.g., ruffles) have a softening effect and tend
  to add fullness to the figure because they add "roundness."
- A *variety of lines* avoids monotony and adds aesthetically
  pleasing designs.
- *Your eye stops where the line stops.* This principle can
  be used to "break up" larger parts of the garment into
  smaller parts, creating interest. It is also used to shorten
  figures. Lines also draw attention to certain parts of the
  garment and body. For example, your eye stops at the depth
  of the neckline, the skirt length, at the rise of the skirt
  slit, or the end of the sleeve. This principle is important
  to remember when practicing modesty. Where do you
  want the eyes of others to stop on your body?

2. PICK GARMENT *SHAPES* THAT FLATTER

The shape of your garment has to do with the outer edge
or silhouette of the garment. Garment shapes tend to follow the
same geometric shapes along women's figures (e.g., hourglass,
rectangle, triangle, and inverted triangle). The latest trends in
fashion impact what shapes you will currently see. It is impor-

tant to remember, however, that not all shapes will be complimentary to your figure. Have you ever gone to the store to try on the latest fashion, but when you tried on garments, nothing seemed to look right? Current fashion does not necessarily flatter everyone's figure. Why do you think they use six-foot tall, underweight women as models? Because they are a blank canvas for any shape. A tall and thin person's silhouette is determined solely by the garment. You must discern what garment shapes compliment your figure. If you have narrow shoulders for example, you might choose to add width to balance out your figure by wearing loose fitting blouses. Remember the eye will follow the shape (or outline) of your garment. Wearing very tight clothing *emphasizes the body part* in the silhouette, *not* the garment.

3. CHOOSE FLATTERING *COLORS*

Color is another powerful element that has the ability to create visual illusions just as lines do. Color has the ability to minimize weight, add height, or draw attention to a particular part of your garment. Here are a few principles to remember with color selection:

- *Light and bright colors* draw attention and increase body size (e.g., red, yellow, royal blue, or orange).
- *Dark and dull colors* minimize size (e.g., black, navy, charcoal grey, olive green, or brown).
- *Dressing in all one color* will make you appear taller because no dividing lines are created by contrasting colors.
- *Contrasting colors* will shorten the figure or divide the figure where the colors meet. Contrasting colors can also be introduced through accessories. For example, selecting a belt of a contrasting color emphasizes the waist area and divides the figure.

- *Two-color outfits* draw the eye's attention to the line where the two colors meet. This principle is especially noticeable with jackets. Here are a few guidelines for selecting jackets:
  a. Jackets are most flattering when they do not end right at the hip line (the horizontal line which adds width across the hip line is generally not flattering to most women). Choose jackets that end right above or right below the hip line.
  b. Jackets that end right below the hip line are usually the most versatile and flattering. They can be worn with dresses, skirts, or pants.
  c. Jackets that end well below the hip line will camouflage the width of hips. Long jackets also appear to shorten the figure—this is good for tall women.

4. SELECT APPROPRIATE *TEXTURES* FOR FABRICS

Texture is the way the fabric both looks (visual) and feels (touch). There are several principles to consider when selecting texture, they include:

- Heavily textured fabrics increase body size as well as conceal the figure shape (e.g., fuzzy sweaters, knobby wool jackets, or deep, pile velvet dresses). Smooth or lightweight fabrics will minimize weight (e.g., crepe dresses, soft cotton blouses, or tan canvas pants).
- Texture reflects light that can make you appear larger (not taller, just larger). For example, a shiny fabric like satin reflects a lot of light and subsequently makes you appear larger. Pile fabrics (like velvet or corduroy) reflect the light and enlarge the figure (that is why darker colors are popular with velvets and corduroy fabrics).
- Texture can be impacted by the weight of the fabric. For

example, a stiff denim skirt that stands away from the body will enlarge the figure. A soft cotton chambray blouse that fits closer to the body will be slimming to the figure.

- Using contrasting textures can create visual illusions (making the top half or bottom half of your figure appear larger or smaller). For example, it is not uncommon to see a lighter colored, textured suit jacket placed with a smooth, dark skirt. For most women, this is a complementary placement of both color and textures.

5. APPLY PLEASING *PROPORTIONS*

Pleasing proportion avoids dividing figures into *equal* halves. While designers often intentionally violate proportion rules in their designs (for example, placing a very short skirt with a very long jacket), these violations usually represent more extreme fashion or fads and generally do not flatter most figures. To avoid dividing your figure into equal halves (50/50) find your "imaginary midpoint" by taking your height and divide it in half; measure up from the floor to locate your halfway point (then avoid clothing that divides you at this point).

6. MAINTAIN *BALANCE THROUGH SCALE*

Balance can be created by maintaining scale in your garments. This means that your clothes should complement the size of your body. This can be applied in two ways. First, select the appropriate size of scale for the prints or patterns in your fabrics. Second, select the appropriate scale for accessories. Tall women can wear a larger scale; while short, petite women should choose smaller scales for fabrics and accessories.

Scale refers to the size of the motif or pattern on a fabric (in other words, how large or small the pattern is on the fabric).

"A pattern is an overall design. A motif is an individual unit of a pattern. Fabric design is often created when motifs are repeated in a prescribed manner to create an overall pattern."[6]

Here are some more tips:

- Plaids come in small, medium, and large scale units. The larger the scale of the unit, the wider the body will look. Small plaid units usually do not adversely affect the apparent size of the small or average-size body. Medium-scale plaids usually can be worn by all, but very large-scale plaids are best suited to the average to tall body type.
- Circular motifs such as polka dots, add width and fullness to the body. Border designs placed at the hemline, waistline, sleeve, or hipline also increase body width.
- Motifs showing a strong vertical movement usually add height to the body, and those showing a horizontal movement usually add width.
- Solid colored fabrics provide the least design distraction and therefore tend to emphasize body shape. In contrast to this, printed fabrics using dull, dark colors will conceal body contours because they "break-up" the body size and provide a distraction to the eye.[7]

"Balance may be defined as equal distribution of weight (actual or visual) from a central point or area. The purpose of balance is to bring into being a satisfying relationship of all design parts. When the design elements: line, form-shape-space, color, and texture are in balance, a pleasing harmony is established."[8]

7. CREATE *FOCAL POINTS*

A focal point is the place your eye is drawn to first. Clothing designers often create focal points through construction details (e.g., decorative collars or gathered sleeves) or through applied ornamentation (e.g., a row of brass buttons or decorative stitching).

Here are some principles to remember:

- If your garment has a focal point built into the garment (like a double-breasted jacket with two rows of buttons) then avoid competing with existing focal points. Instead complement the garment by adding simple accessories, such as a small pair of earrings instead of a large necklace.
- If your garment has no focal point (like a simple black dress), add a focal point through accessories (a necklace, bracelet, pin, earrings, or scarf).
- Remember "less is more" with focal points. You only need to draw attention to one area on the garment. For example, wearing too much jewelry does not emphasize one area and may eliminate the focal point on a garment.
- Focal points attract the attention of the eye (just as lines do).
- The Christian woman needs to be discerning about where the focal point draws attention since she may *not* want the eye to linger there. I would recommend that focal points draw attention to the face whenever possible. Your face is the outward expression of your heart or character—Scripture uses the term "countenance." Your countenance should reflect your hope and joy in the Lord (Psalm 42:11; Proverbs 15:13). The face can become the focal point by:
  a. wearing vertical lines that lead your eye upward through your torso and chest area.
  b. placing light or bright colors on the top of your figure.
  c. adding accessories that keep the focus by your face (e.g., a pin on a jacket lapel); by wearing feminine blouses with collars or other details like gathers, decorative stitching, or tucks.

d. filling in the neckline with a necklace or placing a soft scarf around the neck.

Table 9.1 summarizes the design principles we have discussed. Each woman needs to understand basic design principles and then select garments that help her look her best.

DESIGNING YOUR WARDROBE

For this reason I say to you,
do not be woried about your life,
as to what you will eat or what you will drink;
nor for your body, as to what you will put on.
Is not life more than food, and the body more than clothing?
MATTHEW 6:25

"The average American woman has $2,000 invested in her wardrobe; of that, she wastes 55% of every clothing dollar on unwise purchases and as a result wears 20% of her wardrobe 80% of the time."[9] This is not good stewardship. Our goal when planning our wardrobes should be to meet our needs (and the needs of our family) with the least amount of clothes. How many times have you looked at a closet full of clothes and said, "I don't have anything to wear!" It often feels like this because we have not taken the time to plan our wardrobes. There are several practical steps we can take to help make our wardrobes more versatile and lessen the amount of money we spend on clothes.

TABLE 9.1
PRINCIPLES OF LINE AND DESIGN FOR CLOTHING SELECTION

Short women, 5′2″ and shorter; petite women who desire to appear taller	Tall women, 5′7″ and over, who desire to minimize height	Heavy women who desire to minimize weight	Tall and thin woman who desire to shorten figure and/or add weight
✔Vertical lines that draw the eye up ✔Lightweight, soft fabrics ✔One-color outfits ✔Light and bright colors ✔Small accessories ✔Fabrics with small or medium prints ✔Matching belts ✔Avoid overly long jackets, pants with cuffs, contrasting colors, horizontal lines, and heavy textured fabrics.	✔Garments with horizontal lines ✔Contrasting colors ✔Border prints ✔Fabrics with medium or large prints ✔Large jewelry and accessories ✔Long jackets or low waistlines in dresses ✔Double-breasted dresses or jackets ✔Wide collars or belts ✔Avoid tight or clingy fabrics, short-waisted jackets, short skirts, and vertical lines.	✔Vertical lines (placed close together and not too wide) ✔Dark and dull colors ✔One-color dresses or matching outfits ✔Dull, smooth fabrics ✔Medium scale prints ✔Avoid bright colors, over-scale prints, loose garments, and long jackets.	✔Horizontal lines (created through lines or colors) ✔Over-scale designs or fabrics with large prints ✔Bulky, textured fabrics ✔Light and bright colors ✔Smooth, shiny fabrics ✔Contrasting colors ✔Avoid one-color dressing, vertical lines, and small-scale accessories. Note: Average height women (5′4″ to 5′7″) should avoid extremes in any design element. Select average-scale fabric designs/prints, moderate lines, colors that complement weight.

PRINCIPLE ONE: COMPLETE A WARDROBE NEEDS ASSESSMENT

We often do not wear the clothes we currently own because they are not the type of clothes we wear on a daily basis. You need to consider your lifestyle and then identify the type of clothes you wear for each activity. A sample Wardrobe Needs Assessment Chart[10] is included at the end of this chapter for you to complete (see Table 9.2). Use the chart to identify your various weekly activities and the type of clothing you wear. Categories might include: work, school, casual/at-home, casual/ out, dressy, formal, exercise/sports, sleep. Once you complete the assessment you can compare the clothes in your closet and determine if you:

- Have the right *type* of clothes.
- Have the right *quantity* of clothes for each *category*.
- Have clothes you are *not wearing* at all (you can give them away!).
- Need to *purchase* specific items to "fill-in" holes or *finish off* outfits.
- Need to *update* outfits (through accessories, etc.).

Use the information you gain from your wardrobe needs assessment to make your clothing-shopping list. Carry your list with you when you shop so you can take advantage of sales.

PRINCIPLE TWO: ESTABLISH AND STICK TO A BUDGET

Once you identify your wardrobe needs you can establish a plan for purchasing specific pieces of clothing. I would encourage you not to use credit for clothes, but rather establish a budget and then save toward a specific purchase. Having a budget should help prevent impulse buying, and having a plan should help you purchase clothes that will meet needs. It is recommended that your clothing budget (for your whole family) be 5 percent of your total budget.

PRINCIPLE THREE: FOCUS ON WARDROBE EXTENDERS

Wardrobe extenders minimize the number of clothes needed in your wardrobe. Most of us will not be able to go out and buy a completely new wardrobe every season. So we will need to plan carefully so we can get the most wear out of our clothes. Choose the following for wardrobe extenders:

- *Choose simple, classic styles* since they never go out of style. For example, choose moderate lengths in skirt and jackets, and choose moderate widths in lapels. Items like a simple black dress, a white blouse, a black suit, and tan pants are considered "classics" because they are never out of style.
- *Choose classic colors.* Black and navy blue are two basic colors that you will see every season. Every other color comes and goes in fashion cycles (colors change every six months).
- *Plan around one or two basic color schemes* so you can mix and match your clothes with accessories (e.g., choose black, brown, or navy as a basic color so your accessories, like shoes, will match every outfit).
- *Purchase separates to "update" clothing.* For example, if you have purchased a classic black suit, you can update the look by purchasing a blouse in the latest color.
- *Use accessories to "update" clothing.* New styles of scarves, necklaces, pins, handbags, and shoes can update classic outfits (reflecting current fashion trends).
- *Look for clothing that can be worn year round.* For example, if you purchase a three-piece outfit (skirt, jacket, and pants), it can be worn through all the seasons.

PRINCIPLE FOUR: EVALUATE QUALITY IN CLOTHING

Focus on purchasing *quality* in clothing rather than *quantity* of clothing. Quality clothing will wear better and last longer. Quality clothing tends to be made in classic styles (as we discussed before). To evaluate quality in clothing take time before purchasing each garment to "critique" the construction (look at the stitching, seam allowances, fasteners, etc., to check for quality construction).

PRINCIPLE FIVE: EVALUATE FLATTERING FIT

In addition to the design principles we have discussed, you should evaluate personal fit of the garment. You want each piece of clothing in your wardrobe to be comfortable as well as attractive. Comfort often is associated with good fit (see Table 9.3 at the end of the chapter for questions to help you evaluate good fit).

Once you understand the principles of design and have taken the time to plan your wardrobe, your last step in clothing selection is to understand how to care for your clothes.

CARE FOR CLOTHES

She looks for wool and flax
And works with her hands in delight.
PROVERBS 31:13

The final area we need to discuss related to our clothes is how we can correctly care for them. Proper care for your clothes will extend the life of each garment and ultimately require that you purchase less clothing over the years. Simply put, it's good stewardship to take care of your clothes! The first place to start when caring for your clothes is to establish some kind of plan for caring for them; just as you organize your housecleaning, you need to organize your clothing care needs. I would recommend that you identify all the "jobs" related to clothing care and then establish a plan for when and how you will accomplish each item on your list. See Table 9.4 for a sample list of tasks related to laundry and suggestions for when to accomplish each job.

Once you have organized the tasks related to clothing care, you need to implement your plan—yes, the time always comes when we actually have to wash the clothes! It is important that you understand how to do laundry properly so your clothes will look their best for the duration of the time that you own them. Let's focus on laundry basics.[11]

STEP ONE: READ AND FOLLOW CARE LABELS

Before you purchase a garment you should carefully read the care labels. They give you valuable consumer information regarding the fiber content (cotton, rayon, polyester, etc.) and garment care (e.g., dry-clean only, machine wash, line dry, etc.). Reading the care label may determine whether or not you purchase a particular garment (for example, you may want to avoid "dry-clean only" garments because of the additional care expense).

STEP TWO: SORT CLOTHES CAREFULLY

Sorting separates "like" clothing so the proper washing techniques can be applied. There are several ways you can "sort" your clothes:

a. Sort by colors

Separate loads for whites/pastels/light prints, medium and

bright colors, and finally, dark colors. Remember to always wash new, colored, or dark items separately the first few times because they may fade. This allows you to use the right water temperature as well as proper laundering aides (such as adding bleach to your whites).

b. Sort by fabric or garment construction

Separate clothes that are made from the same fabrics (e.g., separate out towels, cottons, or denims). You can also separate clothes by garment construction; for example, separate loosely woven knits (like sweaters) and tightly woven fabrics (like cottons). This allows you to select the proper washing machine agitation for the type of fabric.

c. Sort by kind and amount of soil

Separate heavily soiled clothes from the general laundry. Substances like mud, oil, or grease require special treatment for stain removal.

d. Sort by size of item

It is a good idea to mix large and small items together because they produce the best washing action and prevent the washing machine from becoming unbalanced during the spinning cycle.

STEP THREE: PRETREAT SOILED OR STAINED AREAS BEFORE WASHING

It is important to treat stains as soon as possible. You may find it helpful to keep a bottle of stain remover by your laundry basket inside the house. I keep a bottle of spray stain-remover in an upstairs bathroom so I can spray stains as soon as my children's clothes are removed at the end of the day (I store it in a locked bathroom cabinet for safety).

Be sure to "test" stain remover on a part of the garment you will not see to make sure the product does not damage the fabric. Also, when treating a spot, be sure to apply the stain remover to the *backside* of the stain. This helps push the stain off the surface, rather than rubbing it in deeper. You have three options when treating soiled garments:

a. Soak

Soaking is generally used for very difficult stain removal jobs (e.g., mechanical grease) and/or sanitizing (e.g., removing body fluids or soaking baby's cloth diapers). Soaking can be done using laundry detergent for thirty minutes, then checking the stain and letting it sit longer (overnight if needed). Presoak products often contain enzymes that are particularly helpful in removing protein-based stains such as blood, grass, and egg. An example of a presoak product is Biz.

b. Prewash

This process "washes" the stained part of the garment before the machine washing. An example of this would be the procedure for removing bloodstains; you run cold water over the stain right away and it "washes" it out.

c. Pretreat stains

This is the most common method of treating stains; simply spray on a stain removal product, allow it to sit a few minutes, and then gently rub the stained area before washing.

STEP FOUR: CHOOSE THE RIGHT LAUNDRY PRODUCT AND FOLLOW THE DIRECTIONS CAREFULLY

Laundering does not work well without the right laundry product. The most common mistake consumers make in laundering is to not use enough of the cleaning product. This results in yellowing, greyness, dullness, and streaks. The manufacturers of laundry products give specific directions based on their testing of the product. There are three main categories for laundering products:

a. Soap

Soap is designed for lightly soiled items and delicate fabrics. It is also used to wash baby items (clothes and diapers), and it works best in soft water. Ivory Snow is an example of a soap product. Note: bar soaps (e.g., Ivory, Camay, Zest, or Coast) can be used for pretreating heavy soils and stains and/or for hand washing delicates like lingerie.

b. Detergent

Detergent is suitable for washing all types of fabrics and stains (lightly stained to heavily stained). Examples of detergents include: Tide, Era Plus, Cheer, Oxydol, Dreft, Bold 3, Gain, Lemon Dash, and Solo. Most of us use laundry detergents rather than soaps because we have hard water (soaps leave a yellow residue on the washer because it reacts with the minerals in the hard water). Liquid detergents (e.g., Liquid Tide or Era Plus) are also effective for pretreating stains. Many laundry detergents contain enzymes which help with stain removal (e.g., granular Tide and Cheer and liquid Bold 3, Era Plus, Cheer, Tide, and Solo). Products containing enzymes can be used as presoaks or stain treatments.

c. Laundering aides

Laundering aides perform specific functions or boost the cleaning power of the laundry detergent. You probably use laundering aides every time you wash—chlorine bleach, fabric softeners, and stain removers are all examples of laundering aides.

STEP FIVE: USE THE PROPER WATER TEMPERATURE

Remember to always check the care labels—they will identify if a particular water temperature is not appropriate. Water temperature aids in the laundering process so you want to select the correct water temperature for the type of fabrics and stains. Here are your water temperature options:

a. Hot water (130 degrees Fahrenheit/54 degrees Celsius)

Hot water does the quickest and best job of sanitizing. Hot water is best for colorfast fabrics, diapers, and heavily soiled items. Hot water will shrink certain types of fabrics—like cotton, wool, and silk.

b. Warm water (90–100 degrees Fahrenheit/32–38 degrees Celsius)

Warm water minimizes wrinkles in permanent press fabrics and reduces the chance of damaging fabrics (e.g., shrinkage, washing out color, or damaging fabrics finishes). Warm water is best for moderately soiled clothes and clothes that are not colorfast.

c. Cold water (up to 80 degrees Farenheit/27 degrees Celsius)

Cold water minimizes wrinkling and fading of colors but does not clean as well. It is best for fabrics that are color sensitive or that will shrink easily (like cottons). It works well for lightly soiled clothes.

STEP SIX: USE THE PROPER WASHING ACTION

The agitation of a washing machine (the moving around of the water, etc.) is equally important to the laundering process as the laundry soaps or detergents. As the clothes are moved around the washing machine, they "rub" or are "agitated" against each other; this is what actually removes the dirt and cleans the garments. Because of this, it is important not to "overload" the washing machine. Select the proper agitation based on the type of fabric and amount of stain (e.g., the washing machine usually has a setting for permanent press or delicates, etc.).

STEP SEVEN: RINSE THOROUGHLY

The washing process loosens the dirt, while the rinsing gets rid of it. It is important to place the appropriate amount of clothes per laundry load so that the washing and the rinsing are able to actually remove the dirt. Rinse in *cold* water regardless of the washing temperature since it does not help further with the cleaning process, it just removes the loose dirt.

STEP EIGHT: DRY CLOTHES PROPERLY

Once again, be sure to check care labels to make sure garments can be machine dried. You may have to lay some garments flat to dry, while other garments may be able to hang dry.

Be sure to check the labels to avoid damaging the garments (e.g., having them stretch out from the weight of hanging or shrinking from the machine dryer). Select the proper dryer temperature (based on the fabric type) to avoid shrinking clothes. Remove the clothes as soon as the dryer stops to prevent wrinkling; you may want to make a note of the time and get there before the dryer actually stops rotating (put a clock by your dryer to help you note the time).

STEP NINE: HANG AND STORE CLOTHES NEATLY

Hanging and folding clothes right from the dryer prepares them to be ready to go back into your closet or dresser immediately from the laundry. Be sure you have the proper type of hangers for your garments.

If you need more specific information on laundry products, stain removal guidelines, or laundry procedures, I recommend that you check out the Web site for the Soap and Detergent Association at www.sdahq.org.

A FINAL THOUGHT . . .

Clothes are a necessary part of life—but they should not consume our lives. Lane P. Jordon provides a fitting conclusion to our discussion on clothing selection; she states:

> Though taking care of our family's clothing needs is important, there are other things that are more important. "Strength and dignity are her clothing" (Proverbs 31:25). Instead of focusing completely on our clothes, we should be concerned with the beauty of our character. We should hope that our inner qualities are obvious to anyone who is with us. The Proverbs woman had this inner strength and dignity that was seen by others. She knew who was in charge

of her life; the Lord. She had an eternal view of life instead of a temporal one. So, she could smile at the future because she knew her life: and the lives of her family were in the hands of God.[12]

May we be women who are clothed in "strength and dignity," women who "smile at the future!"

TABLE 9.2 WARDROBE NEEDS ASSESSMENT							
Time	Sunday	Monday	Tuesday	Wednesday	Thursday	Friday	Saturday
A.M. 6							
7							
8							
9							
10							
11							
P.M. 12							
1							
2							
3							
4							
5							
6							
7							
8							
9							
10							
11							
A.M. 12							
1							
2							
3							
4							
5							

Instructions: Identify the various activities for each day of the week by writing in the type of clothing needed. Total each day to estimate the percentages for each category.

Use your wardrobe needs assessment to evaluate:

- Do you have the right *type* of clothes?
- Do you have the right *quantity* of clothes for each *category?*
- Do you have clothes you are *not wearing* at all? (You can give them away!)
- Do you need to *purchase* specific items to "fill-in" holes or *finish off* outfits?
- Do you need to *update* outfits (through accessories, etc.)?

TABLE 9.3
EVALUATING FIT IN GARMENTS

General Fit

- Is there room for comfortable movement (e.g., standing, sitting, bending over)?
- Are the lines straight (both tight and baggy clothing can create uneven lines)?
- Does it flatter your figure?

Skirts

- Do skirts fit smoothly with enough ease to prevent bubbling under the hips and forming wrinkles across the front?
- Do pleats hang straight and remain closed when standing?
- Is the waistband comfortable but snug enough to hold the garment in place?

Blouses, Jackets, and Coats

- Do jackets or coats fit smoothly over other garments (e.g., blouses)?
- Do collars lay flat and fit closely over the back of the neck?
- Do the sleeves hang straight from the shoulders?
- Are the armholes cut deep enough for comfort?
- Do full-length sleeves reach the wrist bone?
- Do full-length outer coats hang longer than the garments they will be worn over?

Pants/Trousers

- Do pants/trousers fit comfortably over the thighs and calves?
- Are trousers the proper length? (They should touch the top of the shoes or extend one or two inches beyond the shoe top.)
- Is the seat of the trouser comfortable when sitting and standing?
- Is the crotch area wrinkle free?

TABLE 9.4
LAUNDRY SCHEDULE
Daily
✔Empty pockets
✔Check clothing and separate items that need mending or special treatment
✔Put soiled clothing in hamper
✔Air nonwashable items
✔Hang up clothes
✔Pretreat spots and stains as needed
Weekly (or biweekly for larger households)
✔Sort clothes
✔Mend clothes before washing
✔Pretreat spots and stains
✔Hand wash clothes as needed
✔Dry clothes in dryer or air dry
✔Steam press or iron, as needed
✔Fold or hang clothes and store them
✔Take nonwashable clothes to dry cleaner
✔Pick up previous week's dry cleaning
✔Wash bed linens and towels
Occasionally
✔Wash sweaters, jackets, scarves, hats (follow care instructions)
✔Discard or give away clothes that are not worn
Seasonally
✔Wash and store out-of-season clothes
✔Dry clean outer coats and store for next season
✔Wash curtains, throw rugs, pillows, and other washable home furnishings

GROWING IN
DRESSING WITH
DISCERNMENT

1.   *Evaluate your personal views of modesty. Read* Secret Keeper: the Delicate Power of Modesty *by Dannah Gresh (Moody Publishers, 2002).*

      a.   *Evaluate your wardrobe in light of the biblical principles outlined in this chapter.*
      b.   *Are there garments that you should no longer wear?*

2.   *Moms, moms-to-be, and women who want to someday be moms—train and teach your daughters the principles on modesty found in God's Word. You are their first "model" for modesty. How sad it is that so many young women are forced to learn about fashion from magazines, movies, and their peers. Remember teaching and training are two different things. Teaching gives them knowledge, and training gives them skill in decision making. Use the "modesty" principles found in this chapter to develop discussion questions.*

3.   *Apply the design principles discussed in this chapter to complete the chart below to help summarize your personal needs.*

Design Principles and Elements	Application of Principles and Elements for My Figure. (Be sure to consider height and weight also)
Lines and line placement	
Shapes (complementary silhouettes)	
Colors and color placement	
Textures and texture placement	
Body *proportions* and complementary styles	
Scale (fabric prints and accessories)	
Ideas for creating *focal points*	

4. *Conduct a wardrobe needs assessment (using Table 9.2). Identify specific changes you need to make to your wardrobe.*

5. *Organize your laundry tasks:*

    a. Develop a personal laundry schedule using Table 9.4.

    b. Visit the Web site for the Soap and Detergent Association for additional information on stain removal and clothing care at www.sdahq.org.

We began our first book, Becoming a Woman Who Pleases God, *with an account of a young woman who chose to abandon pursuing the study of the qualities that define a Wise Woman because she was not sure that she had an obligation to embrace what was written hundreds of years ago or that she wanted to be SO virtuous. As* Designing a Lifestyle that Pleases God *concludes, I would like to share with you about another young woman who made a different decision. Becky came to the college as an accomplished vocalist who stirred her listeners' hearts with her music. I recall the day she stopped at my office door and asked to talk with me. Quite frankly, I could not imagine why. However, as we chatted I learned that she desired to become a godly woman more than she wanted the acclaim that her musical talent would afford her. She made the difficult decision of changing her major and thus elongating her college education, to acquire the wisdom that could help to mold her into the woman her heavenly Father wanted her to be.*

Today, she and her husband are serving our Lord in a local church where he is the minister of music. Her communications to me, as well as those from her husband, affirm that she made a decision which taught her that . . .

THE WISE WOMAN EXEMPLIFIES SPIRITUAL AND PHYSICAL BEAUTY

Your adornment must not be merely external—braiding
the hair, and wearing gold jewelry, or putting on dresses. . . .
To sum up, all of you be harmonious, sympathetic, brotherly,
kindhearted, and humble in spirit; not returning evil for evil
or insult for insult, but giving a blessing instead;
for you were called for the very purpose
that you might inherit a blessing.

1 PETER 3:3, 8–9

When I shop for clothing or fabric, one of the items I first look at is the label to determine its fiber content and laundering instructions. As a consumer, I expect the label to provide accurate information about the garment's fiber and how to maintain it so I will derive the best performance from it. I also know that the United States government requires all clothing and fabric manufactures to put labels on their products that accurately describe their fiber content, care requirement, and other significant information, such as a flame-retardant treatment for children's sleepwear. I would be upset if I purchased a garment whose label informed me that it was washable only to find that after laundering it according to the instructions, it now fit my 5´ roommate rather than my 5´6˝ frame!

Clothing is a visual description of our character, just as a garment's label explains its anticipated fabric performance. We will be careful to apply the clothing selection principles outlined in chapter nine as we purchase or construct garments if we are seeking to practice the truths of 1 Peter 3:3–4. Likewise, we will be careful to groom our character so that our outward and inward beauty complements one another. Just as the United States government requires all clothing and fabric manufacturers to put accurate labels on their products, so God's Word challenges us to dress in such a way that our outward appearance accurately reflects godly character. Failure to do so sends a conflicting message to others. When I teach this principle to my students, I challenge them with a spiritual grooming activity. For example, I encourage them to record how much time they spend on their spiritual grooming on an average day and to then spend only that amount of time on their physical grooming the following day. What would your grooming for the day look like if you were to complete my project?[1]

A recurring question that the women I talk with have is, "How do I know God's will for my life?" I am amazed that they anticipate a deep theological or even mystical response to come forth from my lips. However, my response is generally something like, "God's will for your life and mine is found in 1 Peter 3:4—we are to do whatever is necessary to cultivate 'the hidden person of the heart, with the imperishable quality of a gentle and quiet spirit, which is precious in the sight of God.'" As John MacArthur elaborates, "*Gentle* is actually 'meek or humble' and *quiet* describes the character of her action and reaction of her husband and life in general. Such is precious not only to her husband, but also to God."[2]

I vividly recall the night I arrived home from a long day on campus and found a Fed Ex tag hanging on my front door. I could not imagine what the package might contain. I investigated the tracking number using my computer and found that it was sent from Chicago. There was only one business in Chicago where I had current contact—Moody Publishers. I signed the tag, giving my permission to have the delivery person leave the package at my home the following day. I approached the front door that evening with *great anticipation!* Lifting the seal of the envelope, I withdrew the contents and my eyes beheld the cover of *Becoming a Woman Who Pleases God.* The first adjective that crossed my mind was *gentle.* From my perspective, the cover designers had captured the intent of the book's content—power under the control of God. Our goal was to communicate biblical truth on how to become a woman who pleases God, *powerfully and gently* inviting the readers to consider the principles. The cover taught me a powerful spiritual lesson: As a woman seeking to please my heavenly Father, I do not have to demonstrate backbone, nor be like a rag doll that flops about. Rather, I am to exhibit strength under the control of the Holy Spirit (Galatians 5:22–23). Such behavior that demonstrates "a *gentle and quiet* spirit, which is precious in the sight of God."

The book of First Peter provides us with principles that challenge us to establish lasting standards of beauty concurrent with the establishment of God's will in our lives. *Principle* is defined as "an accepted or professed rule of action or conduct."[3] Peter not only provides us with *principles* for living out God's will, he also provides us with Sarah as a role model (1 Peter 2:21–3:12). A study of this passage teaches us that Christ is our role model for cultivating a *"gentle and quiet spirit."* Let's take a look at what Peter suggests . . .

PRINCIPLE ONE:
CHRIST IS OUR EXAMPLE
FOR A GENTLE AND QUIET SPIRIT

For you have been called for this purpose,
since Christ also suffered for you,
leaving you an example for you to follow in His steps.
1 PETER 2:21

As Wise Women, our internal thought life, which controls our outward behavior (Philippians 4:8–9), is to reflect that our lives were changed for the better when we were "called" (1 Peter 2:21)—that is, when we became Christians (2 Corinthians 5:17). The liberty Jesus gives us is not license to act as our old nature directs us, but freedom to do what is right (John 8:34–36; Romans 8:1–11; 2 Corinthians 3:17; Galatians 5:1; James 1:22–25). God's Word teaches us that to live under the sovereign control of God, it is necessary to submit to human government and the institutions that He allows to be in existence (Matthew 22:21; Romans 13:1–7; 1 Timothy 2:1–2; Titus 3:1; 1 Peter 2:13). Our Lord modeled this behavior for us when, as the Creator of the universe, He chose to pay the *temple* tax for Himself and Peter (Matthew 17:24–27).

Most importantly, however, our Lord's role model teaches us how to respond to difficult situations. We are to accept patiently any unsought suffering for doing what is right. Contemplate our Lord's lifestyle on earth. His attitudes, speech, response to the needs of people, and the training of His disciples reflected consistent perfection. Then the time came for Him to fulfill His Father's plan. He was to suffer the supreme insult of the cross. Observe His response. When they hurled their insults at Him, He did not retaliate (1 Peter 2:23); when He suffered, He made no threats (1 Peter 2:23); instead He entrusted Himself to Him who judges justly (1 Peter 2:23). "Christ 'handed over' Himself to God, suffering in surprising silence, because of His perfect confidence in the sovereignty and righteousness of His Father."[4] Take a moment to ponder our Lord's response and compare it to yours when a situation that is hurtful to you occurs. Do you find it difficult to keep from retaliating, threatening, and trying to get even? Does your mind phrase comments such as "How could this be happening to me?" or "This isn't fair!"? Or are you willing to believe in and trust the judgment of your heavenly Father, even when you don't understand? Bear in mind that God has no obligation to explain His rationale to us; more than likely, at the time, we would not understand it anyway (Psalm 147:5; Isaiah 40:28; Nahum 1:3).

PRINCIPLE TWO:
DIRECT YOUR ENERGY
TOWARD BEAUTY THAT ENDURES

. . . but let it be the hidden person of the heart,
with the imperishable quality of a gentle and quiet spirit,
which is precious in the sight of God.
1 PETER 3:4

Our attitudes are affected by how we dress. Research studies correlating dress and behavior reveal that the way people dress directly affects their behavior. The Conselle Institute of Image Management teaches, "The way you look directly affects the way you think, feel, and act."[5] Judith Rasband, director of the Institute says, "When you dress down, you sit down—the couch potato trend. Manners break down, you begin to feel down, and you're not as effective."

I am old enough to have lived through the abolishing of dress codes in educational institutions. I can still recall the day the principal of the junior high where I was teaching Home Economics announced to the staff at the end of the year that the School Board had voted to do away with the district dress code beginning the following fall. He further explained that the only items of clothing students were required to wear were shoes because of health codes. He also requested that we not share that portion of the information with the students! I stayed in the junior high environment long enough to watch a significant decline in academic performance and behavior, which I am convinced was due in part to the relaxing of the dress code. When the students in our Home Economics classes present oral reports, they are required to dress professionally—and we provide them with guidelines of what we mean by "professional." Their entire demeanor changes on the days they are professionally dressed.

In Peter's day, as in ours, women put heavy emphasis on their appearance. Peter is not trying to say women should not dress attractively. He is saying, however, that they should not concentrate on making appearance their sole source of beauty (1 Peter 3:3). His illustration of lasting beauty refers the reader to the holy women who did not adorn themselves with the temporal cultural extravagances of their day, but rather with the timeless hope in God that produces beauty of character and disposition (1 Peter 3:4–5). Sarah is cited as an example of a woman who possessed inner beauty, character, modesty, and submissiveness to her husband (Genesis 12:11–20; 1 Peter 3:6).

Customs of dress change almost as frequently as the seasons, and fashions are as fickle as the wind. Any woman who puts her hopes in these to make herself look beautiful will find her standards of beauty constantly changing. Wise is the woman who directs her energy toward her character first and her physical appearance second. This woman will ensure that her beauty will last.

PRINCIPLE THREE:
ALL CHRISTIANS ARE TO LIVE IN HARMONY

To sum up, all of you be harmonious,
sympathetic, brotherly, kindhearted,

and humble in spirit; not returning
evil for evil, or insult for insult, but
giving a blessing instead;
for you were called for the very
purpose that you might inherit a blessing.
1 PETER 3:8–9

As God's children, we are called to live in harmony with one another (1 Peter 3:8–9). This applies not only to husbands and wives but to all members of the body of Christ. In this passage, Peter suggests behaviors for successful relationships among Christians. A number of words and phrases (harmonious, absence of nagging, brotherly, chaste, faithful, forgiving spirit, humble, kindhearted, respectful, and submissive) help us understand what it means to live in harmony. Since it is often helpful to discover more about a word by examining its meaning in its original language (e.g., Greek, Hebrew, Aramaic, Latin), the descriptions below include Greek forms of the English terms:

- *Harmonious* is translated from the Greek word *homophones* and literally means "to be of the same mind." *Be of one mind* is drawn "from two Greek words, meaning 'to think the same,' and 'to be like-minded.' The idea is to maintain inward unity of heart. All Christians are to be examples and purveyors of peace and unity, not disruption and disharmony."[6]
- An *absence of nagging* suggests stillness or quietness. Contention (*paroxusmos*), the source of nagging, implies the action of stirring up or provoking.[7] Nagging is relentlessly bothering another, and a contentious, nagging person distresses others rather than encouraging or affirming them. Women seem to be endowed with a natural tendency for this quality and often behave as if it were a

spiritual gift. Solomon, who certainly possessed a wealth of experience with women wrote, "A foolish son is destruction to his father, and the contentions of a wife are a constant dripping" (Proverbs 19:13); "It is better to live in a desert land than with a contentious and vexing woman" (Proverbs 21:19); and "A constant dripping on a day of steady rain and a contentious woman are alike" (Proverbs 27:15). Elaborating on these verses, John MacArthur shares, "An obstinate, argumentative woman is literally like a leak so unrelenting that one has to run from it or go mad. Here are two ways to devastate a man: an ungodly son and an irritating wife."[8] Wise is the woman who uses *prudence* in her speech, thus exemplifying a quietness and calmness that enriches the lives of those she encounters.

- *Brotherly* is a translation of *philadephoi,* from which the city of Philadelphia derives its name.[9] Throughout First Peter *brotherly* is used to describe the type of relationship that Christians are to have toward one another (1:22; 2:17; 4:8; 5:14). David and Jonathan's relationship give us an example of the brotherly love that our heavenly Father expects His children to have for one another (1 Samuel 18:1; 2 Samuel 1:26–27).

- *Chaste* is not a very popular word in twenty-first-century Christianity. Derived from the Greek word *hagnos*, it implies a freedom from defilements or impurities[10] and is parallel in meaning to *hagios* or holy. As Wise Women, we will choose to develop a chaste character so that our actions are holy and blameless before God (Philippians 2:14–15). I consistently exhort my students that if they are chaste a godly man will chase them! (Read the book of Ruth to see the poignant illustration of this advice). [11]

- *Faithful,* drawn from the Greek word *pistos*, suggests that one is trusted and reliable.[12] When we studied Proverbs

31:10–31, we found that the Wise Woman's husband's trust in her was implicit (Proverbs 31:11). First and foremost, our lives are to be characterized by a faithful relationship to our Lord. Flowing from this will be actions that demonstrate faithfulness, such as keeping promises (Deuteronomy 7:9), obeying our calling (1 Samuel 2:35), using resources wisely (Matthew 25:23), passing on spiritual truths to the next generation (2 Timothy 2:2), and persevering in our faith until death (Matthew 24:13; Revelation 2:10).

- *Forgiving spirit* has as its root *forgiveness*. This "[is] a term denoted in the Old Testament by words that mean 'send away,' 'cover,' 'remove,' and 'wipe away.' In the New Testament 'send away' is used most often; forgiveness is also communicated by words that mean 'loose' (Luke 6:37), 'be gracious to' (Luke 7:43; 2 Corinthians 2:7), and 'pass over' (Romans 3:25). The Bible records human sinfulness, God's eagerness to forgive, and frequent calls by the prophets, Jesus, and Jesus' followers for repentance from sin and return to God."[13] The Wise Woman demonstrates the willingness to forgive others as Christ forgave her (Ephesians 1:7; 4:32).[14]

- Being *humble,* or having humility, is "a value that directs persons to stay within their inherited social status, specifically by not presuming on others and avoiding even the appearance of lording over another. Humble persons do not threaten or challenge another's rights, nor do they claim more for themselves than has been duly allotted them in life. They even stay below or behind their right status."[15] A Wise Woman understands that to achieve *harmony* she is to humble herself. She follows the Lord's example in Philippians 2:8–9 and declares herself powerless to defend her status. Such a response, according to Proverbs 3:34 and James 4:10, is praiseworthy before God.

- *Kindhearted* is a translation of the Greek word *chres-teuomai,* meaning kind, good, and gracious.[16] As Wise Women, we are to be conscious of the distress of others, have a desire to lessen it, and be vessels of God's grace (Proverbs 11:16). Our Lord modeled a heart of kindness through His actions: He healed blind men (Matthew 9:27–30; 12:22; 20:30–34; Mark 8:22–25; 10:46–52; Luke 7:21–22), fed the crowds (Matthew 14:15–21; Mark 6:35–44; John 6:1–4), spoke words of truth to the throngs that followed Him (John 6:22–59; 8:12–47; 10:1–21; 15:1–11), healed people and raised them from the dead (Matthew 8:1–14–16; 19:23; Luke 5:12–26; 7:12–15; John 9:1–7). The healing account in Matthew 9:20–22 is especially poignant for women . . . we complain when our monthly cycle inconveniences us for a brief period of time! This woman experienced an ongoing affliction for twelve years, and it had both physical and religious implications.

  "This woman's affliction not only was serious physically but also left her permanently unclean for ceremonial reasons. This meant all would have shunned her, including her own family, and excluded her from both synagogue and temple."[17]

  His compassionate response to the woman provides a pattern for us—He stopped His activity, addressed her personally, and became actively involved in her dilemma (Matthew 9:22). When we follow our Lord's example we are willing to be inconvenienced by guiding a weak person through a difficult decision, helping a lonely person find friendship, encouraging a sister who is down, affirming someone when she fails, or any other action that reflects kindness.

- *Respectful* is another of the words that twenty-first-century Christians often place in the Victorian category. In our "me first" society, who wants to revere someone else's preferences above her own? *Timao* in Greek means to revere, value, fix evaluation upon, and prize. When we integrate respect into our lifestyle, we choose to consider the words and ideas of others (Galatians 5:13; Ephesians 5:21; Philippians 2:3–4; 1 Peter 5:5), show honor to them, (Romans 12:10–21), and consistently express gratitude (Colossians 3:15; 1 Thessalonians 5:18). I have instructed many students whose parents have trained them to respect adults. One of the ways they often demonstrate their respect to others is by responding to questions with either "yes ma'am," "yes sir," or "no ma'am," "no sir." When they are trained during their childhood, their response is an automatic reflex as young adults; the same reaction should be true in our relationships with others.

- *Submissive* is probably the most unpopular word in the Christian woman's vocabulary. From the Greek *hupotasso,* the word implies a humble surrender to those in authority over us (Romans 13:1; Ephesians 5:21–22; Colossians 3:18; Hebrews 13:17; James 4:7; 1 Peter 2:13; 5:5).[18] The Feminist Movement maintains that if a woman submits to her husband, she loses out on life, gives up her personality, and forfeits her hopes, dreams, and future —all for the sake of a marriage role lived in the shadow of her husband. Regrettably, this philosophy now permeates Christianity. Such a point of view is understandable. A person who knows nothing of the submission of Christ and has never had a positive experience of personal submission would naturally consider submission a sign of weakness. When we see and experience the submission of Christ, we discover that submission is a sign of strength. Submission is not a matter of being forced to yield or surrender to the will of another; rather, it is the deliberate compliance or obedience to the will of another when there is the capability of doing otherwise. As Wise Women, our responsibility is to first have a thorough understanding of the biblical meaning of *submission* (see chapter 3) and then to prayerfully consider whether it is our heavenly Father's will for His daughter to be under another's authority, whether it be employer, pastor, or husband. When we move into a situation with a biblical understanding of *submission* and the confidence that our heavenly Father responded to our prayer with a "yes, proceed My daughter with My blessing," then *submission* will be a joyful, automatic reflex.

Just as the Line and Design Principles discussed in chapter 9 are used to create aesthetically pleasing garments, so the application of Peter's principles to our daily living allows us to design a lifestyle that pleases our heavenly Father! Wise Women will choose to integrate principles that are precious in the sight of God.

MUST I LOOK DOWDY TO BE GODLY?

*Likewise, I want women to adorn
themselves with proper clothing,
modestly and discreetly, not with
braided hair and gold or pearls
or costly garments, but rather by
means of good works, as is proper for
women making a claim to godliness.*
1 TIMOTHY 2:9–10

Dowdy is an adjective that compresses into one word a description of everything that lacks style and color, is out-of-date, and looks shabby. When I discuss fashion with women, I often come across an underlying assumption that if biblical standards of modesty are wholeheartedly embraced, then women are required to eliminate anything fashionable from their wardrobe. Peter is not suggesting that women assume a *dowdy* appearance to be godly. Throughout Scripture we find examples of aesthetically pleasing clothing for both men and women. The garments for the priests were constructed by skilled artisans (Exodus 39:1–31), and the children of Israel were instructed to attach blue tassels on their garments to remind them of their need to trust and obey God's commands (Numbers 15:37–38).[19] Furthermore, our Wise Woman of Proverbs 31 wore garments of fine linen and purple (Proverbs 31:22), the people of Zion were challenged to "awake . . . clothe yourself in your beautiful garments" (Isaiah 52:1), one of our Lord's garments was woven without seam (John 19:23–24), and the attire for the marriage supper of the Lamb is fine linen (Revelation 19:8). What Peter is saying is not to be extreme. Be attractive, but use discretion and dress modestly. Don't let your beauty simply be a matter of outward appearance. Solomon's counsel captures the thought in seventeen words: "As a ring of gold in a swine's snout so is a beautiful woman who lacks discretion" (Proverbs 11:22).

A FINAL THOUGHT . . .

Exemplifying spiritual and physical beauty requires time and effort. To "dovetail" the two, consider using this spiritual grooming routine as you dress daily . . .

As I Physically:	Spiritually I Will:
Cleanse my body	Ask my heavenly Father to create a clean heart and renew a steadfast spirit within me (Psalm 51:10).

As I Physically:	Spiritually I Will:
Apply my foundation	Recall that as God's child I was chosen from the foundation of the world and that my standard of living for this day is to align with His holy standard (Ephesians 1:4).
Accentuate my eyes	Keep my eyes focused on Jesus, the object of my faith and salvation (Hebrews 12:2).
Color my lips	Purpose to say and think those things that are acceptable to my heavenly Father (Psalm 19:14).
Arrange my hair	Recall that my heavenly Father has numbered the hairs of my head (Matthew 10:30).
Put on my garments	Meditate on the clothing of the Christian soldier and purpose to put on the full armor of God today (Ephesians 6:10–17).

As we exemplify spiritual and physical beauty, we will fulfill Peter's instruction of not allowing our adornment to be *merely* external because we have chosen to cultivate the hidden person of the heart, which is precious in the sight of God (1 Peter 3:3–4)!

GROWING IN SPIRITUAL AND PHYSICAL BEAUTY

1. Take a moment to ponder our Lord's role model in responding to difficult situations and compare it to yours when a situation that is hurtful to you occurs.

    a. Do you find it difficult to keep from retaliating, threatening, and trying to get even?

    b. Does your mind phrase comments such as "How could this be happening to me?" or "This isn't fair!"? Or are you willing to believe in and trust the judgment of your heavenly Father, even when you don't understand? Think of specific examples.

    c. Study Psalm 147:5, Isaiah 40:28, and Nahum 1:3. Compare these passages to your response.

    d. Since Christ is our example for a gentle and quiet spirit, use His life as a model for developing goals that will help you to mature the quality of a gentle and quiet spirit in your life.

2. Study in depth the words that define harmonious living (absence of nagging, brotherly, chaste, faithful, forgiving spirit, harmonious, humble, kindhearted, respectful, and submissive) by:

    a. Using the Scriptures, define each term in your own words.

b. *Develop a biblical formula to apply the definitions to daily living relationships. Make the formula practical and support it with Scripture.*

c. *Locate both a positive and a negative example
from Scripture that show how the biblical formula was applied or ignored.*

3. *Analyze the description of the full armor of God
(Ephesians 6:10–17). Align each garment you wear with a
corresponding piece of the Christian's armor. Review the
spiritual "garments" daily as you dress.*

4. *Use Proverbs 31:30, 1 Timothy 2:9–10, and 1 Peter
3:3–5 to develop your definition of biblical beauty.*

5. *Use the following chart to develop your understanding
of how our heavenly Father wants you to groom your
character:*

Daily I Will . . .	
Verse	**Action**
1 Peter 5:5	Clothe myself with humility.
Proverbs 31:25	
Colossians 3:12	
Galatians 3:27; Romans 13:14	
Colossians 3:10	
Ephesians 4:24	
Ephesians 6:11–17	
Proverbs 1:8–9	
1 Peter 3:4	
Colossians 3:14	
Deuteronomy 6:8	

SCRIPTURE GRIDS

The scriptural principles upon which chapters of this book are built are given in the ten Scripture Grids on this and the next several pages.

CHAPTER 1 THE WISE WOMAN'S LIFESTYLE REFLECTS HER HEAVENLY HERITAGE GENESIS 1:26	
Subtitle	**Reference**
A Snapshot of the Wise Woman	Proverbs 14:1
The Wise Woman Pursues Wisdom	Proverbs 4:7
The Wise Woman Is Gracious	Proverbs 11:16
The Wise Woman's Walk	Ephesians 5:15–16
The Wise Woman's Response	Ephesians 4:21–24

CHAPTER 2		
THE WISE WOMAN UNDERSTANDS AND APPLIES		
GOD'S SPECIAL INTRUCTIONS TO WOMEN		
GENESIS 1:27		
Subtitle	**Reference**
The Wise Woman Searches for God's Special Instructions to Women	2 Timothy 2:15–16
The Wise Woman Understands Gender Equity from a Biblical Perspective	Genesis 5:2

CHAPTER 3		
THE WISE WOMAN EMBRACES SUBMISSION		
JAMES 4:6–7		
Subtitle	**Reference**
The Principle of Submission	1 Peter 5:6–7
The Action of Submission	Psalm 138:6
The Obstacles To Submission	Psalm 101:5
Making a Godly Appeal to Authority	Proverbs 16:21
The Results of Submission	Proverbs 16:19–21
Submission for Wives	Ephesians 5:22

CHAPTER 4	
THE WISE WOMAN VISUALIZES	
HER PROFESSION AS A HIGH CALLING	
COLOSSIANS 3:16–17	
Subtitle	**Reference**
The Wise Woman Embraces God's Attitude Toward Excellence	Isaiah 12:5
Walking Worthy of Our Professions	Ephesians 4:1–3
Qualities of the Worthy Walk	Colossians 1:9–10
Keys to the Worthy Walk	Philippians 3:12–14
Who Is Your Role Model?	1 Corinthians 10:11

CHAPTER 5	
THE WISE WOMAN MANAGES	
MOTHERHOOD WITH EXCELLENCE	
PROVERBS 31:28	
Subtitle	**Reference**
The Culture Shock of Motherhood	Jeremiah 29:11
God's View of Motherhood	Psalm 127:3
The Impact of a Mother at Home	Proverbs 29:15
Homemaking with excellence	Proverbs 14:1
Practical Management Tips for Mothers	Titus 2:4–5

CHAPTER 6 THE WISE WOMAN IMPLEMENTS STEWARDSHIP LUKE 16:11	
Subtitle	**Reference**
Practicing Responsible Consumerism	Proverbs 13:11
Distinguishing Between Consumerism and Christian Character	Matthew 6:24
Planning for the Future	Proverbs 21:20

CHAPTER 7 THE WISE WOMAN CULTIVATES A HOSTESS' HEART ROMANS 12:9–13	
Subtitle	**Reference**
What Is the Heart?	Proverbs 4:23
Responding to the Biblical Teaching About Hospitality	Hebrews 13:2
Getting Started	Philippians 3:13–14

CHAPTER 8 THE WISE WOMAN CREATES A BEAUTIFUL HOME GENESIS 1:31	
Subtitle	**Reference**
God the Creator	Genesis 1:1
Understanding Basic Design Principles and Elements	Proverbs 24:3–4
Design Elements	Psalm 19:1
Design Principles	Proverbs 20:12
Creative and Economical Decorating for Stewardship	1 Corinthians 4:2
Living within Our Means	Matthew 6:19–21
Creative Decorating Techniques	Ecclesiastes 9:10
Creating a Warm and Welcoming Home	Proverbs 14:1

CHAPTER 9 THE WISE WOMAN DRESSES WITH DISCERNMENT PROVERBS 31:25	
Subtitle	**Reference**
The Origins of Clothing	Genesis 3:7
Biblical Principles Related to Clothing Selection	Proverbs 11:22
Modesty and the Christian Woman	1 Timothy 2:9–10
Principles of Line and Design for Clothing Selection	Proverbs 31:22–25
Designing Your Wardrobe	Matthew 6:25
Care for Clothes	Proverbs 31:13

CHAPTER 10	
THE WISE WOMAN EXEMPLIFIES	
SPIRITUAL AND PHYSICAL BEAUTY	
1 PETER 3:3, 8–9	
Subtitle	**Reference**
Principle One: Christ Is Our Example for a Gentle and Quiet Spirit	1 Peter 2:21
Principle Two: Direct Your Energy Toward Beauty That Endures	1 Peter 3:4
Principle Three: All Christians Are to Live in Harmony	1 Peter 3:8–9
Must I Look Dowdy to Be Godly?	1 Timothy 2:9–10

NOTES

Chapter 1: The Wise Woman's Lifestyle Reflects Her Heavenly Heritage

1. Pat Ennis and Lisa Tatlock, *Becoming a Woman Who Pleases God: A Guide to Developing Your Biblical Potential* (Chicago: Moody, 2003).

2. J. I. Packer, *Knowing God* (Downers Grove, Ill.: InterVarsity, 1973), 77–80.

3. Tim LaHaye and Jerry B. Jenkins, *Perhaps Today: Living Every Day in the Light of Christ's Return* (Wheaton, Ill.: Tyndale, 2001), 165.

4. Paul J. Achtemier, ed. *Harper's Bible Dictionary* (San Francisco: Harper and Row, 1985), s.v. "gracious."

5. John MacArthur, *The MacArthur Study Bible* (Nashville: Word, 1997), note at Proverbs 11:16.

6. Elizabeth George, *A Woman's High Calling* (Eugene: Harvest House, 2001), 32.

7. I. Howard Marshall, A. R. Millard, J. I. Packer, and Donald J. Wiseman, eds., *The New Bible Dictionary* (Downers Grove, Ill.: InterVarsity, 1962), s.v. "wisdom."

Chapter 2: The Wise Woman Understands and Applies God's Special Instructions to Women

1. MacArthur, *Study Bible,* note at Proverbs 1:7.
2. Joseph M. Stowell, *Strength for the Journey: Day by Day with Jesus* (Chicago: Moody, 2002), 30.
3. "Did They Know?" written by Debbie Ward for a Home Economics course.
4. *Handbook of Accreditation* (Oakland: Western Association of Schools and Colleges, 1982, 1988, 1997).
5. *Standards of Program Quality and Effectiveness in Home Economics* (Sacramento: Commission on Teacher Credentialing, 1996.)
6. MacArthur, *Study Bible,* note at Genesis 2:18.
7. Henry M. Morris, *The Genesis Record* (San Diego: Creation–Life Publishers, 1976), 101.
8. For a sample of *No Turning Back, The History of Feminism and the Future of Women* visit Web sites such as: http://www.news.cornell.edu/releases/Dec98/Friedan.interview.PR.html and http://www.edc.org/WomensEquity/women/friedan.htm to understand Betty Friedan's philosophy.
9. Visit the Concerned Women for America Web site, http://www.cwfa.org/main.asp, to learn more about this organization.
10. A helpful resource is *Portrait of a Foolish Woman* by Nancy Leigh DeMoss. Visit the Revive Our Hearts Web site for ordering information (http://www.LifeAction.org/).

Chapter 3: The Wise Woman Embraces Submission

1. Alexander Strauch, *Men and Women Equal Yet Different* (Littleton, Colo.: Lewis and Roth, 1999), 45.
2. MacArthur, *Study Bible,* note at Ephesians 6:5.
3. Ibid., note at 1 Peter 5:5.
4. Strauch, *Equal Yet Different,* 53.
5. Ibid.
6. P. Bunny Wilson, "Liberated Through Submission," in Nancy Leigh DeMoss, *Biblical Womanhood in the Home* (Wheaton, Ill.: Crossway, 2002), 139–140.
7. Martha Peace, *Becoming a Titus 2 Woman* (Bemidji, Minn.: Focus Publishing, 1997), 134.
8. Nancy Wilson, *The Fruit of Her Hands: Respect and the Christian Woman* (Moscow, Ida.: Canon, 1997), 18.
9. MacArthur, *Study Bible,* note at Titus 3:5.
10. Martha Peace, *The Excellent Wife* (Bemidji, Minn.: Focus Publishing, 1999), 180.

11. John Piper and Wayne Grudem, "A Vision of Biblical Complementarity: Manhood and Womanhood Defined According to the Bible," in *Recovering Biblical Manhood and Womanhood* (Wheaton, Ill.: Crossway, 1991), 55.

12. Ibid., 64.

13. Elizabeth George, *A Woman After God's Own Heart* (Eugene, Ore.: Harvest House, 1997), 75.

Chapter 4: The Wise Woman Visualizes Her Profession as a High Calling

1. *Webster's American Dictionary: College Edition,* 2nd ed., s.v. "profession."

2. Ibid., s.v. "occupation."

3. MacArthur, *Study Bible,* note at Ephesians 4:1.

4. Ibid., notes at Matthew 5:3 and Ephesians 4:2.

5. Ibid., note at 1 Peter 4:8.

6. Ibid., 1826.

7. Charles Hummel, *Tyranny of the Urgent,* (Downers Grove, Ill.: InterVarsity, 1967), 15.

8. See *Becoming a Woman Who Pleases God,* chapter 3.

9. Margery Williams, *The Velveteen Rabbit* (New York: Doubleday, 1958), 16–17.

10. Steve Green, "Find Us Faithful" from *People Need the Lord,* compact disc, Sparrow Corporation, 1994.

11. MacArthur, *Study Bible,* note at Luke 10:40.

12. Arthur Bennett, ed., *The Valley of Vision: A Collection of Puritan Prayers and Devotions* (Carlisle, Penn.: Banner of Truth, 2002), ix.

13. Ibid., 84–85.

14. MacArthur, *Study Bible,* note at Matthew 10:1.

15. Nancy Leigh DeMoss, *Brokenness* (Chicago: Moody, 2002).

16. Ruth White, *Be the Woman You Want to Be,* (Eugene, Ore.: Harvest House, 1978), 94–97.

Chapter 5: The Wise Woman Manages Motherhood with Excellence

1. Reb Bradley, *Child Training Tips,* rev. ed. (Fair Oaks, Calif.: Family Ministries Publishing, 1998), 27.

2. *Thorndike Barnhart Advanced Dictionary,* 2nd ed. (1974), s.v. "excellence."

3. Starr Meade, *Training Hearts, Teaching Minds: Family Devotions Based on the Shorter Catechism* (Phillipsburg, N.J.: P & R Publishing, 2000), 2.

4. *Thorndike Barnhart Dictionary,* s.v. "gracious."

5. Ibid., "encourage."

6. Charles Ludwig, *Susanna Wesley: The Sowers* (Milford, Mich.: Mott Media, 1984).

Chapter 6: The Wise Woman Implements Stewardship

1. Crown Ministries, *Small Group Financial Study,* (Longwood, Fla.: Crown Ministries, 1986), 15.

2. *Thorndike Barnhart Dictionary,* s.v. "conscientious."

3. Roger LeRoy Miller and Alan D. Stafford, *Economics Issues for Consumers* (Belmont, Calif.: Wadsworth/Thomson Learning, 2001), 3.

Chapter 7: The Wise Woman Cultivates a Hostess' Heart

1. MacArthur, *Study Bible,* note at Romans 12:13.

2. *Webster's College Dictionary,* s.v. "teach, teachable."

3. Elizabeth George, *A Woman After God's Own Heart,* 164–165.

4. *Becoming a Woman Who Pleases God,* 37.

5. *Webster's American Dictionary,* s.v. "serene."

6. Ibid., s.v. "spontaneous."

Chapter 8: The Wise Woman Creates a Beautiful Home

1. *Thorndike Barnhart Dictionary,* s.v. "beauty."

2. See *Becoming a Woman Who Pleases God* for additional discussion of these topics.

3. Edith Schaeffer, *The Hidden Art of Homemaking* (Wheaton, Ill.: Tyndale House, 1971), 14–15.

4. John Calvin as quoted by William J. Bouwsma, *John Calvin: A Sixteenth Century Portrait* (New York: Oxford University Press, 1988), 135.

5. Lawrence O. Richards, *Zondervan Expository Dictionary of Bible Words* (Grand Rapids, Mich.: Zondervan, 1985), s.v. "beauty."

6. Terry Willits, *Creating a SenseSational Home* (Grand Rapids, Mich.: Zondervan, 1996).

7. Ibid., 22–23.

Chapter 9: The Wise Woman Dresses with Discernment

1. *Thorndike Barnhart Dictionary,* s.v. "discretion."

2. John MacArthur, *The MacArthur New Testament Commentary: 1 Timothy,* (Chicago, Ill.: Moody, 1995), 78.

3. W. E. Vine, *Vine's Expository Dictionary of Old and New Testament Words,* (Grand Rapids, Mich.: Revell) 1981, s.v. "modest."

4. MacArthur, *1 Timothy,* 78–79.

5. Ibid., 81.

6. Mary Kefgen and Phyllis Touchie-Specht, *Individuality in Clothing Selection and Personal Appearance*. 4th Ed. (New York: Macmillan, 1986), 177.

7. Ibid., 390–91.

8. Ibid., 295.

9. Found at http://www.wardrobemagic.com/.

10. Adapted from the "Lifestyle Chart" Kefgen and Touchie-Specht, *Individuality*, 435.

11. Information for the clothing care guidelines is based on the *How to Clean Kit* by Procter and Gamble (1988). It is now out of print.

12. Lane P. Jordan, *12 Steps to Becoming a More Organized Woman* (Peabody, Mass.: Hendrickson, 1999), 94.

Chapter 10: The Wise Woman Exemplifies Spiritual and Physical Beauty

1. See Sharon Jaynes, *The Ultimate Makeover: Becoming Spiritually Beautiful in Christ* (Chicago: Moody, 2003) for more on this topic.

2. MacArthur, *Study Bible,* note at 1 Peter 3:4.

3. *Webster's American Dictionary,* s.v. "principle."

4. MacArthur, *Study Bible,* note at 1 Peter 2:23.

5. E. Kaplan-Leiserson, "Casual Dress/Back-to-business Attire," *Training and Development,* 54, no. 11, (2000), 38–39.

6. MacArthur, *Study Bible,* note at 1 Peter 3:8.

7. *Vine's Old and New Testament Words,* s.v. "contention."

8. MacArthur, *Study Bible,* notes at Proverbs 19:13 and 27:15.

9. *Vine's Old and New Testament Words,* s.v. "brotherly."

10. Ibid., s.v. "chaste."

11. Helpful resources for chaste include: Elizabeth George, *A Young Woman After God's Own Heart* (Eugene, Ore.: Harvest House, 2003); Dannah Gresh, *And the Bride Wore White: Seven Secrets to Sexual Purity* (Chicago: Moody, 1999); Dannah Gresh, *Pursuing the Pearl: The Quest for a Pure, Passionate Marriage* (Chicago: Moody, 2002); Dannah Gresh, *Secret Keeper: The Delicate Power of Modesty* (Chicago: Moody, 2002).

12. *Vine's Old and New Testament Words,* s.v. "faithful."

13. *Harper's Bible Dictionary,* 1985, s.v. "forgiveness."

14. See "The Wise Woman Develops a Heart of Contentment," chapter 3, *Becoming a Woman Who Pleases God,* for further elaboration on this topic.

15. *Harper's Bible Dictionary,* s.v. "humility."

16. *Vine's Old and New Testament Words,* s.v. "kind."

17. MacArthur, *Study Bible,* note at Matthew 9:20.

18. *Vine's Old and New Testament Words,* s.v. "subject."

19. MacArthur, *Study Bible,* notes at Numbers 15:37–38.

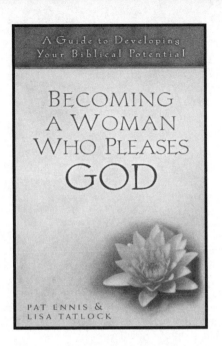

DESIGNING A LIFESTYLE THAT PLEASES GOD TEAM

ACQUIRING EDITOR
Elsa Mazon

COPY EDITOR
Ali Childers

BACK COVER COPY
Becky Armstrong

COVER DESIGN
Ragont Design

INTERIOR DESIGN
Ragont Design

PRINTING AND BINDING
Bethany Press International

The typeface for the text of this book is
Sabon